"A Starr is born! *Don't Forget to Call Home* is a book that offers both a window into the heart of its author and the heart of its reader! Beautifully crafted, original, and anchored in the wisdom of tradition, Rabbi Starr has provided us with a powerful new framework for contemporary theology and the transmission of values from generation to generation."

—ELLIOT J. COSGROVE, rabbi, Park Avenue Synagogue

"Rabbi Aaron L. Starr has hit upon the heart of Judaism, even Christianity, in his bold declaration that God is on our side. Stop thinking God is a punisher who afflicts; God is a companion who upholds. We are here to inhabit that place of blessing, abundance, and possibility. Then, out of overflowing joy, we share this with the world. Mazel tov my teacher, for showing me how to preach the good news!"

—CHRIS YAW, rector, St. David's Episcopal Church

"Aaron Starr has created a book in which finding a personal relationship with God and finding God's presence in our lives seems more than possible. It highlights God's role as our Parent of all Parents with a parent's relevant and meaningful expectations, requiring of us easily achievable honor and responsibilities, all in an approachable and engaging format."

—SCOTT M. NAGEL, senior rabbi, Congregation Beth Ahabah

"Aaron Starr has given us a beautiful way to understand God and God's role in our modern lives. With keen insight and compelling warmth, he empowers us to act in godly ways and to feel God's presence as we are doing so."

—LAUREN BERK___ ___ce president, Rabbinic Initiatives, Shal___ ___merica

D1563614

Don't Forget to Call Home

Don't Forget to Call Home

Lessons from God and Grandpa
on a Life of Meaning

To Dale and Jerry, thank you for being a blessing to the Jewish people and to us. May you and your family know health and hope and much, much joy!

AARON L. STARR

Foreword by Elaine Zecher

RESOURCE *Publications* · Eugene, Oregon

DON'T FORGET TO CALL HOME
Lessons from God and Grandpa on a Life of Meaning

Resource Publications
An Imprint of Wipf and Stock Publishers
199 W. 8th Ave., Suite 3
Eugene, OR 97401

www.wipfandstock.com

PAPERBACK ISBN: 978-1-6667-7440-5
HARDCOVER ISBN: 978-1-6667-7441-2
EBOOK ISBN: 978-1-6667-7442-9

09/05/23

Translations of Scripture passages based on Hebrew text, *Biblia Hebraica
Stuttgartensia*, © 1999 by The Jewish Publication Society.

Translations of the Talmud based on The William Davidson digital edition
of the Koren Noé Talmud, with commentary by Rabbi Adin Even-Israel
Steinsaltz.
License: CC-BY-NC

For our parents
Margie and Jim Starr
Betty and Jim Line
Carol Line (z'l)

For my bride
Rebecca Starr

For our children
Caleb Starr and Ayal Starr

And for Grandpa, Wolf Gruca: We remember.

Contents

Foreword

ELAINE ZECHER

AT WHAT MOMENT DOES growing up turn into growing older?

We spend our early years absorbed in the idea that each year, each birthday, allows us to move closer to that elusive moment of declaring ourselves grown up. And yet, at exactly the moment when that occurs, we begin to grow older. Something happens, however, in the transformation between growing up and growing older. We turn into adults.

And yet, we remain the child of our parent regardless of whatever age we are. We learn what it means as an adult to take on the role of respect and responsibility toward a parent while at the same time asserting ourselves as a grown-up person. How might this awareness lead us to deep and meaningful connection with the Divine?

The answer and exploration lie within the elegant and thoughtful articulation of the pages before you. Within this book, you will not only learn how to be a better parent, aunt, or uncle but also a more loving and dedicated adult child of your own parents. And though this book is actually not specifically designated as a parenting manual, Rabbi Starr provides it as part of the pathway he lays out to understand the role the Holy One of Blessing can have in our lives. If you have never or have ever hesitated to consider that God might be a force in the universe that allows us to discover our best selves through our own agency, then you may be richly rewarded in self-discovery through Rabbi Starr's ability to awaken a capacity you never knew you had. And if you are open to that possibility, then you may find a beautiful elucidation of parenting through the sacred lens of Divine love just as much as you may find Divine love through the sacred lens of parenting.

At its core, this book is about relationships: between us and our children or any children in our lives, between us and our parents and grandparents, and truly, between us and God. These relationships weave a magnificent web of sacred interconnectivity that informs the thoughtful theology presented by Rabbi Starr. Throughout this book, there are echoes of Martin Buber, the twentieth-century philosopher and theologian. His theology brings us closer to the powerful image of relationship articulated in these pages.

Martin Buber described three specific kinds of relationships.[1] He taught that we have a utilitarian kind of interactions where we objectify the other for their purpose to serve us. Buber called this an "I-It" encounter. In essence, we fail to see the humanity, the real person behind the job or activity another is providing for us. But there are also moments and encounters that transcend and transform one another to more deeply understand to appreciate the existence and dignity of another. In this way, we relate to each other through a sacred prism. God becomes present between us. Buber called this "I-Thou." When we understand that there are respectful and loving ways to relate to another, then it is also possible to regard the Divine in a similar manner.

The Bible and rabbinic texts teem with examples of how the relationship between parents and children and vice versa create encounters that provide positive and negative models of connection. Parenting has its moments of utilitarian purpose, with and despite great love. Providing for children demands great dedication and commitment. Likewise adult children and our relationships with older parents call upon us to serve them and provide for their needs, through a lens of respect and understanding. And

1. See the book *I and Thou* by Martin Buber.

in return, those parents of adult children employ their agency to love us while letting us grow independent of their watchful presence in our lives. These relationships as described in this book play an important role in developing the kind of theology Rabbi Starr helps us understand.

Rabbi Starr offers elucidating textual references that move the reader through growing up and growing older and the relationships that surround these transitions. He then delivers us into a model and metaphor of God as a watchful yet somewhat removed parental image who needs and expects us to express our relationship by "calling home." Just as we know how important it is to maintain our connection as adults to our parents by calling home, Rabbi Starr transforms this image by helping us understand and embrace the idea that we can connect to God through actions of faith by engaging in lovingkindness and justice. This is how we spiritually "call home." God becomes much more accessible than we could have ever imagined as adult children of the Divine.

The essence of this book finds its foundational core in the humanity of its author. Aaron Starr is a beloved rabbi, devoted husband, nurturing father, dedicated son and grandson, and a Jew who loves Judaism. You will discover the beauty of his soul throughout the stories and teachings he elegantly presents and teaches. From 2019–2023, I had the privilege of being his study partner, his *hevruta*, as part of the Shalom Hartman Institute's Rabbinic Leadership Initiative. Together we delved into texts of Jewish tradition, parsing the verses and arguing over their meaning. My appreciation of his scholarship and commitment to the Jewish people and world at large grows stronger with each study session. I'm grateful for my own growth through our many sessions in person and on Zoom together. The presence of God has moved through us and with us, and for this, I feel blessed.

You will feel God's presence, as well, as you make your way through Rabbi Starr's story and his ability to bring ancient ideas into the twenty-first century, a new and ageless way of living life with meaning and sacred purpose through a divine lens of love, set forth on the pages before you.[2]

---

2. Rabbi Elaine Zecher is senior rabbi of Temple Israel of Boston. She edited *Because My Soul Longs for You: Integrating Theology Into Our Lives*, CCAR Press, and is a Senior Rabbinic Fellow of the Hartman Institute.

Acknowledgments

THIS BOOK IS TWENTY years in the making. My rabbinate is of course shaped by my seminary training at the Hebrew Union College—Jewish Institute of Religion. More recently, my fellowship with the Shalom Hartman Institute has inspired me and nourished me, deepening and reinvigorating my leadership in profound and meaningful ways.

I am tremendously grateful to my colleagues and friends who teach me and guide me daily, and I am blessed to learn and to laugh with so many talented teachers and deep souls who honor me with their friendship. I count too among my friends and teachers so many people throughout the Metro Detroit Jewish community and especially the members of the two synagogues I have served during my rabbinate: Congregation Shaarey Zedek in Southfield, Michigan—my home since 2008—and Congregation Shir Tikvah, where I spent the first four years of my career (and where I grew up, too). Thank you for allowing me to share my wisdom, and thank you for sharing your wisdom and kindness with my family and with me.

I am grateful to those whom I trust to improve my writing and who critique my words with love: Marla Morgen, Larry Nemer, Leah Gawel, Rick Cohen, Sheldon Jacob, David Cuttner, Elise Gechter, Rabbi Adam Baldachin, and others. Any mistakes in this text are absolutely my own; any wisdom and insights come from the opportunity given to me to stand on the shoulders of giants, including those who help me to clarify my teachings with constructive criticism. I am thankful also to Catherine Bell, who encouraged me to make the time for my joy in writing; to Joshua Bilmes for his advice; and I am grateful too for the friendship, encouragement, and support of Rabbi Elaine Zecher, Rabbi Lauren Berkun, Rabbi Elliot Cosgrove, Rabbi Scott Nagel, and Father Chris Yaw. It has been a pleasure working with and receiving support from Wipf and Stock, including Christopher Klimkowski, Emily Callihan, Rachel Saunders, Matthew Wimer, and George Callihan.

Words cannot describe my gratitude for my family: those to whom I was born and those to whom I am connected through marriage. I can only speak of God as a loving Parent because I am the son and son-in-love of five people who show me what it means to give fully of myself to others while also allowing those whom I love the freedom to live their own lives. Our parents are my teachers and a constant source of love and support.

Moving through the family tree, I am blessed by amazing children who allow me to grow and who help me to grow—while sustaining me with their love, their light, and their laughter. In so many ways their intelligence, humor, kindness, forgiveness, and respectful nature make parenting easy (easier, anyway).

Most of all, I am grateful to my bride of more than two decades, Rebecca, who is in all ways my teacher and my best friend. Whatever good I might do in this world starts with her support and encouragement and continues with her advice, wisdom, hard work, and care. "Many women have done well, but you surpass them all" (Prov 31).

And I am grateful to you for reading my words and for allowing me to share my thoughts. Please, let me know your reactions to the ideas in this book. When you share your thoughts with me, you too become my teacher. "Who is wise?" Ben Zoma asked. He answered himself: "One who learns from all people" (Pirkei Avot 4:1).

The goal of this book, ultimately, is to deepen our relationship with God. So, I will conclude here with the words of my mother-in-love of blessed memory, Carol Line, who often said in good times and in difficult ones, "God is good."

A Note on Translations and God-language:

All translations of the Hebrew Bible and rabbinic writings are my own and are meant for the sake of understanding rather than literal, word-for-word translation. I chose to render God's four-letter proper name, the tetragrammaton, as ETERNAL. For Jews, God's name is ineffable, and the pronunciation lost to history. However, God's name is a combination of the conjugations of the verb "to be," which is to say, embedded in the name is the idea that God was, God is, and that God always will be. Therefore, God's name indicates that, indeed, God is ETERNAL.

In addition, I work hard to avoid ascribing God a gender. Occasionally this makes for clunky English and for that, I am sorry. I do try to avoid English pronouns in referring to God and instead simply replace what otherwise would be a third-person pronoun by again using the word God. It is redundant but since God is incorporeal, any gendered language with regard to God is entirely inaccurate.

Introduction

I AM THE GRANDCHILD of Holocaust survivors. As a child, seeing the numbers tattooed on my grandmother's arm, I began wondering about God's seeming absence from 1939–1945. How could the God who rescued the Israelites from slavery in Egypt thousands of years ago remain silent while six million parents and children, siblings and friends, were murdered?

My mother's mother, Regina, was born in Krakow, Poland. The Nazis and their accomplices murdered my grandmother's parents and siblings. She survived because of her training as a seamstress, and thus her utility as slave labor. My grandfather, Wolf Gruca, was born in Czestochowa, Poland. The Nazis and their accomplices murdered my grandfather's parents and siblings, along with his siblings' spouses and their children. He survived the war because of his training in tool and die, and thus his utility as slave labor.

My grandparents met after World War II in a displaced persons camp in Germany. After a short time, they married; they had a child; and they moved to the United States where, with just a little help from distant relatives and the support of the Jewish community, they built a life, and they grew their family. My grandmother died when I was twenty-three years old, near the end of my first year in the seminary. My grandfather survived and even thrived for another twenty years, seeing his grandchildren married and giving him great-grandchildren.

Near the end of my grandfather's life, he asked me the question directly: "Rabbi," he lovingly called me, "where was God?"

I wanted to quote the experience of Elijah the Prophet: "There was a great and mighty wind, dividing mountains and breaking boulders by the power of the ETERNAL; but the ETERNAL was not in the wind. After the wind—an earthquake; but the ETERNAL was not in the earthquake. After the earthquake—fire; but the ETERNAL was not in the fire. And after the fire—the sound of a quiet calm" (1 Kgs 19:11–12).

Instead, speaking as a grandson who for years has searched to reconcile faith with the existence of evil and suffering, I replied, "Grandpa, I don't know."

This book is an attempt to answer his question, "Where was God?" even though, ultimately, my answer remains, "I don't know."

This book is also a reflection on my own and other's relationships with aging parents. My parents are a huge help in my life. From holiday celebrations to driving carpool, and from sitting side-by-side in the synagogue to hosting our children for joyful overnight stays, they are helping us to raise our family and to build our careers. We, as their adult children, value them tremendously for that. Likewise does our synagogue—our house of worship—value them and other retirees for their time, their efforts, and their generosity. In this way and other ways, our aging parents are transformational in building lives, in building families, and in building communities. They offer their adult children and each other wisdom, love, support, and a pair of helping hands.

Unfortunately, the world in which we live often seems to place less value on these contributions to society than it places on those who build companies and strengthen the economy, or those who entertain us through music, movies, television, and athleticism. As such, the young are often seen as more useful than the old. Moreover, it is said that, beginning in the nineteenth century and then snowballing into the twentieth century and today, for the first time in world history, children know more than their parents. This is often true in technology and in industry. The result is an unprecedented devaluation in the role of the aged within society.

Sacred scripture, however, tells us just the opposite. "Remember the history of the world; understand the generations gone by; ask your parent so that they will tell you; your elders so that they will share with you . . ." (Deut 32:7). Among my goals in this book is to remind the young and old alike of older adults' transformational role in helping to elucidate the meaning and purpose of life.

Lastly, this book is a meditation on parenting and the age-old struggle to understand our evolving role as parents in each stage of our children's lives. Rebecca and I are blessed with two wonderful boys quickly becoming outstanding young men. Since the moment they were each born, I wanted to wrap them in Bubble Wrap and lock them in the house to prevent them from encountering the inevitable cruelty, suffering, sickness, and setbacks that life often brings. After all, to a certain extent, my job as their father is to protect them.

Somehow, almost contradictory, my job as a father is also to send them off into the world to live their own lives: to fall in love, to achieve success, to grow, to journey, to blossom. Parenthood, then, requires not the offering of permanent shelter and impermeable shield, but the teaching of skills for our kids to acquire their own food, water, and shelter; to cope with vulnerabilities and inevitable failures; to carry on the task of building a more just and compassionate world; and to be able to build meaningful lives of gratitude, obligation, and joy. Our job is to help our children to achieve independence so that each year they need less of us.

Parenting is an ever-changing two-step in offering protection and freedom, wisdom and silence, discipline and praise, all in the name of love. For us, parenting is an imperfect two-step, but the intentions are always for the best, and I hope that our children will honor our intentions, forgive our imperfections, and maintain a relationship with us even as we age.

When our kids were little, Rebecca began a tradition of them calling their grandparents every Friday to wish them a Shabbat shalom: a peaceful Sabbath. When I praised her for this beautiful idea, she sweetly admitted that it was not entirely altruistic: "When our kids move out of the house and when they have kids of their own too," Rebecca explained, "I hope that they will stay in touch with us. We still will have much to offer them, and even more, we will need their love and support too."

Perhaps we strive to understand God as our Parent who, while remaining ever present for wisdom or encouragement and hope, has sent us as adults out into the world to succeed and to make a difference. God is quietly cheering us on, hoping that we remember God's expectations of us to practice gratitude; to fulfill the obligations of pursuing justice, acting with kindness, and to take care of our brothers and sisters; and to live meaningful, joyful lives. That is, after all, part of our mission: gratitude, obligation, joy . . . and then there is one more thing that God and that our parents as well ask of us: to call home.

This book offers one way in which we might perceive God in the twenty-first century. Perhaps even more, this book offers a reflection on one's relationships to aging parents. Probably most of all, this book is a meditation on parenting and the age-old struggle to understand our evolving role as parents in each stage of our children's lives.

This book is divided into three sections. The first section, "Seeking God, Understanding God," presents some of the more traditional theologies of the Western world as well as the question of theodicy: why bad things happen. The second section, "God Wants Us to Lead a Meaningful Life," explores the expectations that God, as our Heavenly Parent, is placing on us. The third section, "But Don't Forget to Call Home," presents some thoughts on what we might expect from God and how we can benefit from investing in our relationship with the Divine.

With that, I turn back to the question my grandfather asked and the question I am often asked as a rabbi: Where is God in our most challenging moments? Where was God during the Holocaust?

"I don't know, Grandpa, how God allowed the Holocaust to happen. I don't know how God allows any suffering to occur to good human beings. But I believe that God gifted humanity free will, and with that free will, I think that God wants us to lead lives of gratitude, obligation, and joy." After all, God gave us the tools to do just that. And even with our free will, I believe that God still has much to offer us and needs something from us too: No, God doesn't need us to care for Him/Her the way aging parents might need from their children. Rather, God needs us from generation-to-generation to carry forward God's hope of perfecting the world in which we live. God also needs us to be in relationship with Him/Her. In this way, our lives are imbued with meaning and purpose, and they are made all the richer when we don't forget to call home.

Seeking God,
Understanding God

1

God Is Our Empty-Nester Parent

WHEN WE BECOME ADULTS, we often gain a deeper appreciation for the wisdom our parents possess and for the hard work they put into parenting. Despite my accusations against them to the contrary when I was a teenager, now I can acknowledge my parents' successes in raising children. First, they gave my brother and me food, clothing, and shelter. Second, they taught us strong values and made sure that we received a good secular education too. Third, they ultimately allowed us to leave the house to become productive members of society. And lastly, without meddling and without imposing themselves, they are available for wisdom or for a helping hand any time of the day or night.

Especially as a teenager and even now as an adult, whenever I part from my parents they always kindly request: "Don't forget to call home." They allow me my freedom and independence, but they also want to know that my travels, by car or by plane, were safe and successful. They want to know that my family, friends, and I are alright. I'm sure, too, that they probably just want to hear my voice one more time. "Don't forget to call home" is a simple request for assurance and love.

Of course, as the father of teenage boys, I am just starting to really understand how hard of a job this "parenting thing" is. With our own children, my wife, Rebecca, and I are long past diaper changes and kissing boo-boos. On more than one occasion, after being ignored by one child or told by the other child that I was wrong, I actually lamented to them, "It is amazing that when I am at the synagogue (as its rabbi), a goodly number of people think that I know something. The moment I come home, however . . . I know nothing." As my children are getting older, I have come to realize that it is not parenting that is actually so hard—after all, the bulk of parenting is driving your kids to and from school, sports, and friends' houses; making them do homework and eat their vegetables; and trying to help them apply the lessons today that we taught to them when they were in kindergarten about being good people, working hard, and making choices that strengthen them and their future, as well as our community and our people. Now that we are the parents of adolescents, though, I have come to see that the hardest part about parenting is actually learning when *not* to parent: when to let go and when to allow our children to fail in order to learn for themselves. The hardest part about parenting is learning when to step back and to keep our mouths shut.

Giving children roots requires hard work; allowing them the wings to fly, however, and giving them the space to do so requires tremendous acts of faith. We allow our kids to leave the proverbial nest, of course, but whenever my sons get on airplane for some faraway destination, or even when my sixteen-year-old drives somewhere new for the first time, I ask, "Don't forget to call home."

Adulting

When I was eighteen years old, I went to my parents and asked them to allow me to go on a high school senior year spring break trip in which we would drive from suburban Detroit all the way south to Orlando, Florida. I planned to drive down there along with seven other teenagers for a week's vacation. To my relief at the time, my parents acquiesced; my parents actually said "yes."

4

Looking back on that conversation now, as a parent of a teen driver, I think that my parents must have been out of their minds. How in the world did they summon the courage to let me go: eight teenagers on a road trip from Michigan to Florida? And yes, they instructed me as I left, "don't forget to call home." And I did.

Then, a few days into the trip, I called them from Florida once again; my dad picked up the phone. "Dad! Guess what I just did? I went sky diving!"

There was a pause on the other end of the phone, and, to this day, I remember my father's words distinctly: "Aaron, you jumped out of a perfectly good airplane?"

"Yes," I responded.

"And you're safe?" he asked.

"Yes," I responded.

Another long pause. "Must've been quite a trip down." My father would've been justified in yelling at me, in calling me foolish or perhaps a different, more colorful adjective. But he did none of that. He celebrated with me. It became a beautiful moment between father and son.

Later, however, my father revealed another reaction. In that phone call, my dad realized that I had grown up. I had called him *after* the fact to revel in the joy of my experience and not *beforehand* to ask for permission. My parents and I had entered the next stage of our relationship. Though I was not able to understand it at the time, in allowing me to succeed and to fail on my own—in giving me the power of my own freedom, they had to figure out how to let go; how to step back; how to withhold their own power and wait to be needed. And for me, well, it took me decades after that incident to realize how brave and how wise they were to allow that development to happen. As I said, giving children roots requires hard work; allowing them the wings to fly, however, and giving them the space to do so requires tremendous acts of faith.

No matter our age, we continue to have much to learn from our parents, and even more to gain from maintaining a healthy relationship with them. In addition to all that for which we are grateful to our parents, we acknowledge how the parent-child relationship changes from when we were young to when we became adults. We honor our parents' wisdom and abdication of authority in allowing the relationship to change: how they knew when to give money but not advice or when to give advice but not money; how they knew when to speak and when to keep silent; how they knew when to volunteer to help and when to step back to let us succeed or even to fail; how to be present but not in the way. We know too that when we suffer, our parents suffer; and that when we succeed, our parents revel in our success. They could not and cannot solve all our problems, but they could and still can be our great support: either in this world or from the heavenly realm. We know also that parenting is hard and imperfect—it can be at times painful and messy, exhausting and infuriating. We are mature when we can forgive our parents' shortcomings[1] and when we acknowledge our own. We also know that parenting is holy and sacred, full of love and laughter, and we work hard to make sure that those are the memories that carry forward.

God as Heavenly Parent: Humanity in Its Childhood

I imagine, too, that God faces the same challenges that we parents do. According to Genesis, God provided Adam and Eve with everything: food, clothing, and shelter, and these early humans were told to remain in that infantile state by avoiding the fruit of the tree of knowledge of good and evil. Perhaps this request, however, was harder than it sounds.

The Bible says that on the sixth day of creation, God brought humanity into the world through the power of words. "Let us make humankind in our image, as in our likeness," God seemingly says to no one in particular (Gen 1:26). Rabbi Moses ben Nachman—known by the acronym "Ramban"—explains the "us" in this declaration to include earth; in other words, just as the earth brought forth animals on the previous day of creation, so too does God use the earth to bring forth humanity as well. After all, the

---

1. Shortcomings are different than abuse. In the case of an abusive parent, our reaction to the abuse can and should be different.

first person created receives the name "Adam" from the *adamah*, the Hebrew word for earth or soil.

By contrast, the great Bible commentator Rabbi Shimon ben Yitzchak—known by the acronym "Rashi"—teaches that "let us make man" refers to God sharing the Divine's plan with the angels. From this, Rashi derives a lesson: those with greater power should consult and include those with lesser power in their decision-making. Unlike Ramban who suggests that the "us" of "let us make" is God and the earth, Rashi teaches that "us" is God and the angels.

Personally, my preferred explanation for "Let us make man in our image" is that God consulted not with the angels nor with the earth, but rather with the animals which God created on the fifth day. As a result, then, humanity is part divine and part animal: in rabbinic terms, *yetzer hatov* and *yetzer hara*. Our soul is the *yetzer hatov*, the "good inclination," encouraging us to reach morally and ethically for the highest of principled behavior. At the same time, we are in possession of the *yetzer hara*, the "evil inclination"—the animal instincts which require us to eat, to sleep, to desire, to covet, to compete, to procreate, to war, and more. It is this combined divine-animal soul that ensures "to everything there is a season" (Eccl 3:1). Throughout most of human history, God set upon humanity the challenge of finding balance between the *yetzer hatov* and the *yetzer hara*. We possess the free will to choose between good and evil, right and wrong. We are empowered to aspire toward the spiritual or to succumb to our basest "animal" instincts.

Of course, we do not hold children to the same expectations as adults when using their free will to make constructive choices. Their brains lack the ability to consistently make higher level reasoning and to think beyond themselves. We are born self-centered. The younger we are, the more our *yetzer hara*—our animal needs—dominate our thinking. A hungry baby who wakes in the middle of the night is not concerned for his or her mother and father's well-being; otherwise, they would just let us sleep already! It takes a human up to twenty-five years, along with lots of teaching, mentorship, successes, and failures, to develop the ability to truly think beyond the particular moment in which we are living, to see and to act beyond our own needs and desires.

And that is just to develop the *capacity* to achieve higher-ordered thinking, not the actual achievement of it! For many of us, it actually takes much longer to consider others before ourselves. If the average American lives into his or her seventies or early eighties, that means one-third of our lives is spent in this period of self-centeredness. There is a reason that we cannot legally drive until we are sixteen; that we cannot vote or serve in the military until we are eighteen; that we cannot drink alcohol until we are twenty-one; and even that, in America at least, certain positions of government are off-limits until we reach a prescribed age.

In this way too a Jew is not subject to the *mitzvot* (commandments) of Judaism until one is thirteen for a boy (bar mitzvah) and twelve (or in some communities, thirteen) for a girl (bat mitzvah). Traditionally, when one becomes bar or bat mitzvah, a parent recites over the child a prayer of thanksgiving: "Thank you (God) who released me from being punished for this child." That is to say, prior to the age of responsibility, a parent is required to ensure that his/her child is behaving appropriately. Thereafter, a child becomes an adult: responsible for the decisions s/he is making for herself/himself. Of course, in our own time, a parent continues to be responsible for the decisions of a child for many more years after that child becomes bar/bat mitzvah, but the prayer is a recognition that a child cannot be held responsible until reaching a certain developmental stage of life.

When Adam and Eve were brought into this world, they were in many ways like children before the age of responsibility. They acquired food with little effort (Gen 2:15 and 3:17–19). They lacked any sense of time beyond their own wants and needs; it seems that they could not understand that life was finite (Gen 2:17 and 3:19) and, depending on how one reads the text, God might even have given them a chance at achieving immortality (Gen 2:9). Adam and Eve knew no sense of power or powerlessness (Gen 3:16). They experienced no shame or embarrassment (Gen 2:25 and 3:10–11). Perhaps most of all, they lacked an understanding of "good" and "bad." It seems too that God desired humanity to maintain this profound, childlike innocence and naivety and thus prohibited Adam and Eve from consuming the fruit of the tree of knowledge of good and bad (2:17). I am reminded of the wisdom my sister-in-law offered us whenever we complained about one aspect or another of tending to our children when they were tiny: "Little children, little problems; big children, big problems." It is only when our children grow older do we gain perspective on the scope of the challenges they—and thus we—face!

The biblical story of Adam and Eve tells us that, at creation, God felt a closeness to humanity like a parent holding close a new-born child. Often a child grows more quickly than a parent is willing to accept. We appeal to our children, "You will always be my baby!" as we hold them tight, sometimes even as we hand them the car keys or when they are rocking children of their own. The Bible seems to indicate that Adam and Eve were already at the point of creating a separation from their Parent well before God was ready for that separation to occur.

Like a parent, then, who brings forth life into this world and instinctually wants to provide for her child's every need and to protect that child from every possible harm, God brought forth humanity into this world with the highest of hopes and the best of intentions. God sought to provide us with everything and to protect us from every threat. Like most children, though, Adam and Eve chose to do the one thing that they were specifically asked not to do. They ate from the fruit and then they denied their wrongdoing. In punishment, God's children were then put into "time-out"; God expelled God's children from the garden.

Humanity in Its Adolescence

Not surprisingly, Adam and Eve's children fared equally poorly. Both Cain and Abel wanted to please their Heavenly Parent. In the first but not the last example of parental favoritism, God noticeably preferred one child over another: God accepted Abel's sacrifice over Cain's. Cain became so distraught in his jealousy of God's favoritism toward Abel that Cain rose up and killed his brother. Knowing something was wrong, our Heavenly Parent called Cain out, testing the child by asking Cain where his brother Abel was. Cain responded, "Am I my brother's keeper?" (Gen 4:9). So incensed that Cain would ask a question whose obvious answer was an emphatic "Yes, you ARE your brother's keeper," God banished him into exile: Cain was forced to roam the earth, homeless. And perhaps, as Rabbi Dani Siegel comes to teach, the entire Bible is God's affirmative answer to the question, "Am I my brother's keeper?"

Future generations continued to fail their Heavenly Parent and God's punishment of those children grew more severe. By the time Noah came around, the Torah tells us that humanity had grown increasingly violent and licentious; thievery was commonplace too. During that period, God made a difficult determination about the nature of humankind: "The ETERNAL saw how abundant humankind's wickedness was on earth, and how each machination of his mind was simply evil all the time" (Gen 6:5). We know what happens next. No metaphor for parenting explains the great destruction that took place in the days of Noah: God grew so angry at humanity that our Heavenly Parent wiped out an entire generation and started over. Of course, God lamented the decision that needed to be made: "And the ETERNAL found comfort that [God] had made humankind on earth (as opposed to the heavens), yet [God] regretted (the decision to create humanity with all its imperfections)" (Gen 6:6).

When God destroyed the generation of Noah, God seemed to think that a reboot on humankind would eliminate the potential for violence, licentiousness, and thievery. Yet immediately after the flood, even Noah and his children strayed from what one might identify as a path of purity. So, like a parent who discovers the essential nature of her child and changes the educational system rather than trying (yet again) to change the child's nature, God shifts gears in how God wants to set humankind on the path toward righteousness.

With the story of the Tower of Babel coming on the heels of the story of Noah and his children, Genesis transitions to a genealogy that leads directly to Abraham. In so doing, it seems that God saw the wisdom in appointing role models for humanity, and so, because of their profound aptitude for faith and innate sense of justice and of righteousness, God chose Abraham, Sarah, and their descendants to serve as teachers and role models of justice and righteousness.

Unfortunately, the descendants of Abraham and Sarah were themselves imperfect and, even more so, faced a daunting task in trying to right the behavior of a human species obsessed with strength and power. Society continued to devolve.

> Then arose over Egypt a new king who did not know Joseph. [This new king] said to his people, "Behold, this nation of the people Israel is greater and stronger than we are. Let us act shrewdly toward it, lest it grows even larger; in the event of war, it will join forces with our enemies in fighting against us and [we Egyptians will be forced] to leave this land."
>
> So [the Egyptians] set taskmasters over [the nation of Israelites] to punish them with suffering; and [the Israelite nation] built supply cities for Pharaoh: Pitom and Ra'amses. Nevertheless, the more [the Egyptians] punished the nation of Israel, the more it increased and spread out, so that the [Egyptians] came to loathe the Israelites. Then the Egyptians hardened [the Israelites'] labor ruthlessly. [The Egyptians] embittered their lives with heavy labor at mortar and bricks and with all sorts of tasks in the field. All this work with which [Egyptians] tasked [the Israelites] was done with ruthlessness. (Exod 1:8–14).

In Pharaoh and the Egyptians' fear of the "other," the Egyptians enslaved the Israelites and caused them terrible suffering. The Heavenly Parent saw Her firstborn child (Exod 4:22) suffering and decided to act. God sent terrible plagues against the Egyptians, and God empowered the Israelites with the leadership of Moses, Aaron, and Miriam. Eventually Pharaoh relented and sent the Israelites toward freedom until Pharaoh realized the gravity of that decision.

So, with the Egyptians pursuing us, God rose up like a protective parent to defend a threatened child; the Torah tells us that in that moment God appeared as a warrior to cast Pharaoh's army into the sea (Exod 15:3). Our Heavenly Parent rose to our defense when we could not protect ourselves.

As biblical history continues, God's relationship with the people Israel changes frequently. Like the parent of an adolescent, God sometimes deals with childish behavior and other times God responds to our growing maturity. When God gave us the law at Sinai, for example, God appeared as a wise, old man—a beloved grandfather, perhaps—granting us wisdom and instruction. Still later, when the Babylonians were sacking the Holy Temple and destroying Jerusalem, the early rabbis perceived God as an angry, violent parent: a judge on high punishing us for our misdeeds. For many of us, these are the images that we still hold of God: the warrior; the wise, old man; the stern lawgiver; or the judge on high punishing us for our failure to live up to covenantal standards.

A Time to Speak and a Time for Silence? The Growing Separation Between God and Us

In turn, by the talmudic era, our rabbis offered different images of God in order to explain our suffering. We read in one teaching that God is depicted as an elderly person: powerless, impotent, unable to protect her children.[2] This new image of God suggests a role reversal whereby the child now supports the parent. In other words, it is our job to support God as one cares for an elderly parent. Many have been down that road before, an adult child supporting an aging parent; you might be walking it now or soon: trying to the best of your abilities to maintain dignity for your parents while recognizing that a role-reversal has occurred.

How do you imagine God? Or, perhaps more to the point, is that image of God representative of what we need of God today? The warrior; the wise, old man; the stern lawgiver; or the judge on

2. Mishnah Brachot 9:5.

high punishing us for our failure to live up to standards? Do you perceive God as an aging parent in need of support? A child needs a parent, sure—a parent who is loving but strict, who provides warmth but also structure. At some point, though, the parent-child relationship evolves. Indeed, the world of the Jews changed two thousand years ago; the stern Parent's stick seemingly struck us too hard, and we could not rationalize that the punishment fit whatever sins we had committed. Exiled from our land, abused by one nation after another, we began to question how a loving God could treat the favored child in this way. So that we might learn? We had learned. So that we could be a light unto the nations? Surely there were other ways. In our own lives and in our own times, how are we to understand God?

When the Children Become the Adults

In turn, I would like to suggest that God is not the judge on high writing and sealing in a book of life and death, whose hands are involved in every detail on earth. God is no longer the warrior who casts our enemies into the sea. Rather, perhaps God is the Parent who, while remaining ever present for wisdom or encouragement and hope, has sent us as adults out into the world to succeed and to make a difference. God is quietly cheering us on, hoping that we remember God's expectations of us to pursue justice, to act with kindness, to live meaningfully, and to take care of our brothers and sisters. That is, after all, part of our mission: pursue justice, act with kindness, live meaningfully, take care of our brothers and sisters . . . and then there is one more thing that God—and that our parents, by the way—ask of us: to call home.

So it is, then, that as adults, we put our own actions under the microscope. What is it that our parents taught us? What legacy did they hope that we would carry on? Are we living in such a way as to bring honor to our parents' names? I would imagine that part of their wisdom—their demand of us—would include the same expectations that God has of us: "Be grateful. Remember your obligations to pursue justice, to act with kindness, and to take care of your brothers and sisters. Live meaningfully and joyfully . . . and don't forget to call home." Then, when we transition from young adulthood to older adulthood, we learn that the value in calling home is not just for God and not just for our parents; it is for us too.

Our job is to be the adults that our parents and that God want us to become—to live in such a way as to bring to their names honor and blessing. And our job is to remember to call home as often as we can. As we read in Psalm 145, "the ETERNAL is near to all who call upon God . . . to all who call upon God in truth." Like our parents, God too is here for us. Always. Though perhaps now as older, wiser adults, we will call home for advice *before* we jump out of a perfectly good airplane.

2

What Does God Do?

As one grows older, belief in the Creator—the Heavenly Parent, the ETERNAL, the Rock—often takes on greater significance. We start to accept that our own sense of power is overinflated and that there must be something else in control. Or, just as there are no atheists in foxholes, so too are there few atheists in hospital beds. Our own vulnerability and awareness of life's finitude often propels us to believe in a God that acts in our lives—that has the power to heal and to grant an unending, pain-free existence (or what might be termed "heaven"). Such a faith also often rests on a belief that there is a continuity to the world; that we are part of something bigger than ourselves. We yearn to believe that there is a plan to the seeming chaos we see around us and that, whether in this life or in heaven, the good will be rewarded and the bad will receive their justice. More to the point, as we read in Joshua 1:9, our faith provides us with a foundation upon which to "be strong and courageous." Then, as Joshua encourages, and as our faith reminds us, "do not be afraid; do not be discouraged, for the ETERNAL your God will be with you wherever you go."

The Bible promises us a God who acts within history and who interacts with individuals. At the same time, we accept that God is not a vending machine that receives our prayers and automatically spits out whatever we desire. Many believe that God acts; God just does not *always* act. So what is it, then, that God does?

God as Creator

Our ancestors were vastly more in touch with the natural world than are many of us living in modernity—we whose eyes are drawn more frequently to a television, cell phone, or computer screen. Our ancestors attributed the beauty and orderliness of earth and its natural laws to God as a grand architect for all creation. In fact, the rabbis teach that among the first things that God created was the Torah itself, and that God then used the Torah as a blueprint for the rest of creation. Genesis tells us in its opening verse, "When God began to create the heaven and earth, the earth chaotic and unorganized with darkness over the surface of the deep and a wind from God sweeping over the water, God said, 'Let there be light'; and there was light" (Gen 1:1–3).

Likewise, Psalm 93 praises God as Creator: "Nature stands firm; it cannot be shaken. Your throne stands firm forever; you have existed always. The oceans sound, ETERNAL: the oceans sound their thunder (and) the oceans sound their pounding. Above the thunder of the mighty waters, more majestic than the breaker of the sea is the ETERNAL, majestic on high" (Ps 93:2–4).

But far from resting on heavenly laurels, the Psalms also come to tell us that God renews the work of creation daily. In Psalm 104 we read, "The One who sends springs through the ravines; between the hills they go, giving drink to all the wild beasts; the wild asses slake their thirst. The birds of the sky dwell beside them and sing among the foliage. You water the mountains from your lofts; the earth is sated from the fruit of your work."

The Bible then explains that not only did God create *ex nihilo* (out of nothing) but that God also spent time ordering creation. God creates and, just as important, God also turns chaos into structure and form. God likes an organized world in which each aspect of creation has its place and its ways. Psalm 104 continues:

You are the One who causes the grass to grow for the cattle, and [creates] fields for man's labor that he may bring forth bread from the earth. [You are the One who produces] the wine that humankind enjoys, oil that makes their faces shine, and bread that sustains a person's life. The trees of the ETERNAL are satiated, the cedars of Lebanon, God's planting, are where birds make their nests; the stork has her home in the junipers. The mountain heights are for wild goats; the cliffs provide shelter for the hyrax. God made the moon to mark the seasons; the sun knows when to set. You bring on darkness and it is night, when all the forest animals move about. The young lions roar for prey, seeking their food from God. When the sun rises, they gather in their dens to rest. Humans go out to work, and labor until the evening. How abundant are the things you have made, ETERNAL! With wisdom, you have made them all; the earth is full of your creations. (Ps 104:14–24)

Yes, God likes a world of rules, of submission, of cause and effect. God likes a world in which creation obeys God. For the believer, the very presence of the natural beauty around us testifies to God's existence and handiwork, and the laws of nature celebrate God's commitment to orderliness. Again, from Psalm 104: "All of them look to you to give them their food in its season. You give it to them, [and] they gather it up; you open your hand, [and] they are well satisfied. [When you] hide your face, they are terrified. [When] their breath expires, they perish and return to dust. You send your breath anew, they are created, and you repair the face of the earth" (Ps 104:27–30).

The theology of Psalm 104 among others tells us of a God who is daily involved in our lives as a provider—as a Parent providing nourishment for every fruit of the divine womb. Psalm 145, one of the central prayers of the Jewish prayer book, is even more direct with God's role, giving thanks to God for what God does for humankind: "The ETERNAL supports all who stumble and raises all who are bent. The eyes of all look to you with hope, and you give them their food in its season. [You] open your hands, satiating the desire of all that lives" (Ps 145:14–16).

God as Caretaker

These psalms speak of God as abounding in kindness, forgiveness, mercy, and love. They tell us that God is caring for us every day, providing for our every need. Psalm 147 goes even further in describing what God does, speaking of God's daily activities toward nature, toward animals, and even toward end-times prophecies:

> The ETERNAL rebuilds Jerusalem; [God is the One who] gathers in the exiles of Israel. [God is the One who] heals their broken hearts and binds up their wounds. [God is the One who] counts the number of the stars and names each of them. Our Master is great and powerful; there is no accounting for God's wisdom. The ETERNAL gives courage to the lowly and brings the wicked down to the dust. Sing to the ETERNAL . . . who covers the heavens with clouds, provides rain for the earth, makes mountains put forth grass; who gives the beasts their food, to the raven's brood what they cry for. (Ps 147:2–9)

In a beautiful story from the Talmud,[1] God spends each day caring for those most in need and, in this way, God serves as a moral exemplar for each person. What does God do? God clothes the naked (Gen 3:21); God visits the sick (Gen 18:1); God consoles mourners (Gen 25:11); and God ensures the proper burial of the deceased (Deut 34:6). In so teaching, the rabbis suggest that beyond the act of renewing creation each day, God is busy caring for humankind the same way that God cared for our biblical ancestors.

In our earthly lives, the best example of one who creates, provides, and heals is a parent. A mother and father give us life. A mother or father ensures (or ought to ensure) that we have food on our plates and a roof over our heads. A mother or father kisses boo-boos, gives us medicine, takes us to the doctor, teaches us about eating healthy, and holds us when we are in pain. Jewish tradition teaches that visiting one who is sick takes away 1/60 of that person's illness simply by the presence of the visitor;[2] all the

1. b. Sotah 14a.
2. b. Ned. 39b.

more so does the presence of a loving parent lessen the suffering of a sick or scared child.

But our parents' lives are finite. So it is that we read in Psalm 27: "Though my father and mother abandon me, the ETERNAL will take me in. Show me your way, O ETERNAL, and lead me on a level path because of my watchful foes. Do not subject me to the will of my foes, for false witnesses and unjust accusers have appeared against me. Had I not the assurance that I would enjoy the goodness of the ETERNAL in the land of the living. . . . Hope in the ETERNAL; be strong and of good courage! Hope in the ETER-NAL!" (Ps 27:10–14).

Similarly, we read of God referring to the people Israel as "my child, my firstborn, Israel" (Exod 4:22). Or, as we read in the book of Isaiah, God assures the prophet, "Like a person whom his mother comforts, so shall I comfort you" (Isa 66:13). For children, there is very little more reassuring than the loving embrace of a parent. So too, for believers in the midst of a difficult situation, faith provides comfort. God creates; God provides; and God heals.

In 2007, my mother-in-law Carol died one month before our first son, Caleb, was born. One can imagine the bittersweet joy we experienced as my wife Rebecca went into labor. Just shy of two weeks after her due date, I was on a bike ride with my father-in-law when I received a call from Rebecca to come home. Her water had broken! We made it to the hospital with no problems and settled into our room. The *Lord of the Rings* trilogy was on, so we prepared for the inevitable waiting that often comes with childbirth. Twenty-five hours later—yes, twenty-five hours later (including watching the entire trilogy, by the way)—our beautiful son was born. They placed that bundle of joy into my arms first and, overwhelmed with emotion, I thanked God with a traditional Jewish blessing: ". . . *shehechyanu vikiy'manu vihigianu lazman hazeh*: Thank you God for giving us life, for sustaining us, and for allowing us to reach this sacred moment in time." Of course, right after saying this special blessing, I uttered additional words of "holiness." The second thing that our firstborn, Caleb, ever heard, after *shehechyanu*, was the University of Michigan's fight song, "Hail to the Victors."

Rebecca and I were on top of the world. Another twenty-five hours passed, though, and I went from thanking God to pleading with our creator. Rebecca experienced respiratory distress from an allergic reaction to some medication the hospital had given her; I raced into the hall looking for help and the first face I saw "happened" to be Rebecca's doctor making her rounds! I rushed into the room. In those scary moments of fear for my wife's life and wonder at how I might raise a child by myself, I prayed to God with all my being that God might protect us with a divine sheltering presence. As medical intervention allowed the crisis to pass, I once again thanked God for the gifts of life and health. After all, God is the healer of broken hearts (Ps 147:3).

When times are at their most difficult, we want and even need to believe in a God who will intervene in our individual lives. That said, there are risks to God watching every move. There are consequences to attributing everything to the work of God's hand.

3

What Does God Do? Part II

GOD CREATES; GOD PROVIDES; and God heals. Does God punish, too?

Go Forth! God as the Parent of Teenagers

As God seeks to move humanity from infancy (the naivete of Adam and Eve) to toddlerhood (the jealousy of Cain toward Abel) and into adulthood, it is necessary for a third stage: the teenage years.

Parenting Teenagers

Teenagers possess an incredible capacity for personal responsibility. Indeed, after many years working with teens, I know well that when tasked with a particular assignment, a leader will often emerge among a group of teenagers to usher his or her friends toward a shared goal. When properly inspired, those friends too will rise to the occasion and own that which is delegated to them.

At the same time, teenagers possess an incredible propensity for self-assuredness. They know everything and they are not afraid to tell you; teenagers often believe that they possess all the answers. Teenagers often dismiss the advice of older adults in order to pursue their own paths. Sometimes they—and at points in life, all of us—need to make mistakes before internalizing important lessons and truths. And this brings us to the patriarch Abraham.

"Go forth," God commands Abram (later to be renamed Abraham) seemingly out of the blue. God then promises Abram land and family: security today (land) and security forever (family). Abram is told that he will function as a mirror for the world's behavior: those who bless Abram will in turn be blessed; those who curse Abram will in turn be cursed. Abram/Abraham, without question, accepts God's mandate. Who is Abraham that God would select him for this unique place in the movement of the world from chaos to order, from violence to peace, from self-centeredness to love for others?

Genesis itself offers us little about Abraham's childhood. Like a teenager, Abraham acquiesces at times to his Heavenly Parent's demands, and, at other times, Abraham asserts his qualified independence.

Rather, we come to see that the man who would seemingly accept without objection God's command to leave everything he knows and then later to offer his son up for sacrifice is committed in his core to the idea of justice.

In Genesis, we hear the voice of God seemingly speaking to no one in particular but explaining the Divine's special relationship with Abraham. "I have given him special attention," God announces, "because [Abraham] will instruct his family and his descendants to keep to the path of the ETERNAL by practicing righteousness and justice, in order that the ETERNAL may bring about for Abraham that which [God] has told him" (Gen 18:19). God then reveals the plans to destroy the cities of Sodom and Gomorrah on account of their residents' failure to uphold the important nomadic value of welcoming guests into their homes.

In the ancient world, especially as nomads crisscrossed the fertile crescent of the Middle East, the difference between life and death often came down to the hospitality of others. Abraham and Sarah proved themselves to be just and right when they welcomed the three men (later to be revealed as angels) into their tent. The residents of Sodom and Gomorrah did the opposite: rather than welcome these strangers and offer them food and drink, they sought to abuse the strangers in their community. In this often-misunderstood story, the great sin of Sodom and Gomorrah, in fact, is their failure to practice kindness toward the stranger.

Upon hearing God's plans, Abraham immediately begins his negotiations. God accedes to Abraham's pleading, agreeing that if God found even ten righteous people in the cities that God would spare them the divine wrath. The irony, of course, is that in God's omniscience, *of course* God knows what the results will be. That piece of the story is actually secondary. Rather, there are two significant lessons that come out of this particular story.

The first important piece of information that we learn is about Abraham and his willingness to call God out for that which he (Abraham) perceives as wrong. In one of the most powerful lines in five books of Moses, Abraham yells at our Heavenly Parent, "That's sacrilege! For you to do such a thing (as destroy Sodom and Gomorrah), to bring death upon the righteous along with the wicked, so that the righteous and the wicked are alike. Sacrilege! Will the Judge of all the earth not act justly?" (Gen 18:25). God chose Abraham, we learned a few verses earlier, because of Abraham's commitment to justice and righteousness. Abraham has the *chutzpah* to challenge God on the values that God holds most dear.

The second interesting piece of information that we learn from this encounter between God and Abraham is that God is willing to work in a mentor/mentee relationship with Abraham. Like the parent of teenagers, God understands the value of incorporating Abraham into the heavenly plan. If Abraham and his descendants are going to follow in God's footsteps, then they need to understand God's values and God's expectations.

With Abraham as our example, we too are justified in questioning why bad things happen to good people. Moreover, we are obligated to question the seeming injustice that pervades our world. We too are required to ask if all that happens—the good and the bad—are truly products of God's will.

In Isaiah (45:7) we read of God, "I form light and create darkness. I make peace and create wickedness." The framers of the Jewish prayer book struggled too with this idea, taking from Isaiah but amending his words for use in the morning prayers, "I form light and create darkness. I make peace and create *everything*." Perhaps centuries ago, God, as the Parent of an infant humanity, became involved in every aspect of life including bringing justice to evildoers and even taking credit for the evil these people performed. As the grandchild of Holocaust survivors, however, and even with the birth of the State of Israel some three years after the end of World War II, I challenge the notion that God continues to be involved in every aspect of humanity.

I cannot accept that God would allow the suffering of so many millions of innocent people. Rather, I think that, over the centuries, God has stepped back. I believe that as humanity evolved and systems of justice improved over time, God is now allowing us as adult children to live our lives. Justice and righteousness are no longer in the direct hands of God; they are now in our hands. God has become the Parent of adult children.

Biblical Theology #1: God Sends Plagues as Punishment and as Messages

It is true that the Torah presents many examples of God using nature against humankind and it is tempting therefore to view the world today through these radically ancient lenses. Early in Genesis, because of society's violence, corruption, and unwillingness to treat each other with radical and even unmerited kindness, God sends the flood waters against the generation of Noah and rains fire down upon Sodom and Gomorrah. The plagues God sends forth on Egypt are used by God both as a punishment against the

Egyptians for oppressing the Israelites and as a message to the Israelites of God's awesome power. It's no coincidence that a careful look at the text, though, reveals that God carefully selected the natural phenomena that the ancient Egyptians worshiped as gods and used those phenomena as a punishment and as a message that all nature is subservient to the One creator.

The Torah mentions many other plagues as well. For example, in Exodus, we read the story of the Israelites rebelling against God and Moses by worshiping the golden calf. "Then the ETERNAL struck the people with plague," the Torah explains, "on account of what they did with the calf that Aaron made" (Exod 32:35). Deuteronomy explains that if we love God and if we serve God with all of our heart and soul, then God will grant us rain for the land in its season and crops in our field (Deut 11:13–21). If we worship other gods, however, God will turn away from us and "will shut up the skies so that there will be no rain and the ground will not yield its produce" (Deut 11:17). Indeed, the Torah makes clear that God punishes those who rebel against God and rewards those who follow our Creator.

It is easy and sometimes comforting to view the world in this way. By attributing everything to divine will, it gives us a sense of order, stability, and purpose in this world. On the other hand, viewing the world through this lens also leads us to view those who suffer as somehow "deserving" of their fate. As we grow older—as we see more of the world and look more critically at how it operates—we learn that suffering and sinning do not always correlate. The people who die in earthquakes, hurricanes, tornados, and tsunamis, among other natural disasters, do not deserve their deaths.

Biblical Theology #2: The Suffering Servant as a Light unto the Nations

As the centuries passed, theology evolved. While the prophetic literature never calls into question God's ability to use the natural world as a punishment or as a message, it also reminds us that "bad things happen to good people" *even though* they are "good" and not because of some fault in their behavior. The prophet Isaiah comes to teach a concept called "the suffering servant," which is to say, perhaps the righteous suffer as a means by which God can teach the world. More to the point, Isaiah shows that the experience of suffering facilitates our ability to serve as a light unto the nations (Isa 42:6).

Perhaps the most extreme example of this theology (which I vehemently oppose but which some people believe) might suggest that the Jews warranted suffering the horrors of the Holocaust. I remember exactly where I was sitting when I engaged a colleague in a discussion of God's seeming silence in the midst of the Shoah (a reference to Job, this is the Hebrew term to describe what in English we call the Holocaust) of World War II. My colleague then asked earnestly, "Aaron, where was Reform Judaism born?"

"Germany," I responded, not sure where exactly he was going.

"And Aaron, where was the Holocaust born?"

Again, I responded, "Germany."

"Exactly," my colleague replied. He went on to tell me that God was not only punishing those who ceased observing the commandments, but God was also teaching a lesson to the rest of us about the "sin of assimilation." I abhor such victim blaming and reject such a line of thinking.

If the five books of Moses suggests that God punishes the wicked, the prophetic literature adds that God sometimes also causes suffering not because of the fault of an individual or a community, but instead in order to teach certain lessons to others. And perhaps that explanation is well and good thousands of years after a tragedy, but if we believe in a benevolent God, it is awfully hard to justify God causing the suffering of some of God's children just to teach a lesson to others of God's children.

An idea similar to that of the suffering servant is what the rabbis who most certainly knew from suffering came to call "chastisements of love."[1] Rabbi Joseph Soloveitchik of blessed memory summarized this notion of "chastisements of love" when he wrote, "Afflictions come to elevate a person, to purify and sanctify his

1. b. Ber. 5a

26

spirit, to cleanse and purge it of the dross of superficiality and vulgarity, to refine his soul and to broaden his horizons."[2]

For those who subscribe to the idea of "chastisements of love," it is not others who learn from one's suffering; rather, the person who experiences the suffering is challenged to take lessons from the suffering. This rabbinic idea further suggests that temporal suffering serves to cleanse the soul in this world and thus, when one dies, any suffering experienced on earth expedites the sufferer's passage to heaven. One who embraces the notion of "chastisements of love" might even celebrate the experience of suffering because of the reward waiting on the other side.

When Theology Hurts

In my mind, it's easy when one is young and healthy to believe that God is benevolent, omniscient, and omnipotent. It's easy when we live in America in the twenty-first century with a roof over our head, three meals a day, and as much clean drinking water as we want, to believe that God is both all-good and all-powerful and that God interacts daily with our individual lives: to reward us or to punish us, to teach us or to inform others. But what happens when our lived reality differs from the biblical theology of God as abounding in kindness and acting with an outstretched arm? When one's health is threatened; when one faces profound loss; when one is lacking adequate food, water, and shelter; or when one is facing oppression, persecution, and murder: How, then, do we begin to understand God?

Still trying to explain why God's chosen people could experience such suffering, Elie Wiesel in the book *Night*,[3] his classic work about the Holocaust, brings the metaphor of God's powerlessness to its logical conclusion when he wonders whether God was swinging on the gallows alongside the Jews at Auschwitz. How else, Wiesel posits, could our Heavenly Parent be so seemingly

2. Soloveitchik, "Kol Dodi Dofek," 56.
3. Wiesel, *Night*.

silent in the wake of such suffering? With the Jews at their very lowest, perhaps, as Nietzsche argued, God *is* dead. In those moments of the Holocaust and immediately thereafter, we Jews felt orphaned, parentless, bereft of the rock upon which we so heavily leaned. I empathize with how the victims and survivors of the Holocaust might feel that way; when suffering occurs on any level, the lack of explanation is bewildering; heartbreaking; infuriating; crushing. At some point in time, many of us question God's intentions or even God's existence.

I too struggle with the mystery of how our loving Parent could allow such suffering. As was written by an unknown individual on the wall of a cellar in a Cologne concentration camp, "I believe in the sun, even when it is not shining. I believe in love, even though I don't feel it. I believe in God, even when God is silent." I too believe that even when we fail to fully understand God's ways, that God is not acting through some heavenly-ordained punishment. I believe.

Somehow, out of the ashes, the Jewish people rebuilt and now we Jews today, both in America and in Israel, are more successful than perhaps at any other time in world history. Yet, despite our successes, there are no recorded ruptures in natural law, no strong hand and outstretched arm, no cloud of glory by day and pillar of fire by night that can explain away our success as some overt heavenly miracle. Even as a believer, though—as someone with faith in God and who sees in twenty-first-century Judaism the continuation of the covenant that goes back to God and Abraham, Isaac, and Jacob—none of the traditional paradigms for understanding our relationship to God seem plausible to me. Rather than the overt miracles of biblical times, God instead seems to be working through individuals: whether they be national leaders like David Ben Gurion and Yitzchak Rabin, or communal leaders like those who step forward as synagogue presidents, agency executives, volunteers, clergy, educators, and Jewish professionals.

I believe that God is working through each of us when we listen to God's teachings and strive to live God's laws. We are more than three-quarters of a century after the Holocaust, one of if not the worst tragedies to ever befall the Jewish people. We are also three-quarters of a century after one of the greatest events to happen to the Jewish people in the birth of the State of Israel and we are experiencing in America greater social acceptance, economic success, and communal strength than anywhere in the last two thousand years. Given the juxtaposition of the great tragedy and the great successes, how might we then understand our relationship to God today?

As the grandchild of Holocaust survivors, I come face-to-face with the theologically complicated intersection of blessing and curse. In Deuteronomy (32:4), we read, "A God of faithfulness without injustice, righteous and fair is God." These are the words Judaism invites us to pronounce as we lay a loved one into their final resting place. And these are the words denied to my grandparents not only in the murder of scores of their relatives during World War II, but these words are the core of a faith denied to countless survivors and their descendants since the Shoah, who cannot with a whole heart proclaim: "A God of faith without iniquity, righteous and fair is God."

For half of my grandfather Wolf Gruca's life, he understandably challenged the notion of God as "righteous and fair." After all, how could a God "righteous and fair" allow the murder of my grandfather's parents, siblings and their spouses, nieces, nephews, aunts, uncles, and cousins? How could a God righteous and fair destroy Grandpa's Jewish community in Czestochowa, Poland? How could a God righteous and fair allow the genocide of six million Jews? How could a God righteous and fair allow a father to tell his son, as my great-grandfather holding in his hand only his tallit (prayer shawl) and tefillin (phylacteries) while awaiting the trains told my grandfather, "Son, I will never see you again"? How could a God righteous and fair allow my grandfather to survive, but not his older brother who had accompanied Grandpa through so much of his time at the camps?

A Holocaust survivor is justified in questioning the attribution to God the qualities "righteous" and "fair," and Wolf Gruca's frustrations with our Creator did not cease when Grandpa came to the golden land of America. After all, how could a God righteous and fair allow my grandparents and their young son to arrive on the shores of this great country only to be ushered into a makeshift apartment building repurposed as a shelter for the homeless? How could God strike Wolf's wife, my grandmother Regina, with a debilitating muscle disorder that robbed her of her ability to move and forced my grandfather seven days a week to work caring for her at home by night just as hard as he worked on the floor of the Chrysler Assembly plant by day? For more than seventy-five years my grandfather Wolf Gruca carried the heavy burden of survivor's guilt and, with it, the struggle—the brokenheartedness—in the thought that the faith that had brought him such joy as a child could be based on the entirely false premise of God's goodness.

Like water that can over time reshape even stone, seventy-five years of living as a survivor can ultimately bring healing and change perspective. Toward the end of his life, my grandfather's faith returned to him. As a centurion looking back on his life, Grandpa began to uncover the hidden hand of God guiding him. In hindsight, Grandpa believed that it was God's help that allowed him to pass a test of life and death: reading the blueprints forced upon him by a Nazi commander and written in a language my grandfather did not speak, Grandpa correctly interpreted those blueprints, whereby the Germans determined my Grandpa could be useful to their efforts and thus worthy of saving. In hindsight, my grandfather believed that the hidden hand of a righteous God was at work when Grandpa's lifelong dislike of dairy allowed him during the war to trade his small ration of butter for a little extra bread. My grandfather believed in hindsight that it was the righteous God who gave him the strength to jump from a moving train to transfer from a British controlled zone for displaced persons to an American one, where he ultimately met Regina, the woman to be my grandmother. My grandfather believed in hindsight that it was the hand of a righteous God that kept alive my uncle, then a tiny preemie that could fit in the palm of your hand, through the challenges of the displaced persons camp and then a journey to America.

In the last twenty years of his life, and not in hindsight but in real time, my grandfather beheld the righteous hand of God when one of his grandsons became a rabbi, and even more so, when that grandson assumed a position at a large, prestigious synagogue. My grandfather believed that it was the hand of God that helped him to find love again after the passing of my grandmother, and after barely surviving the war and losing so many loved ones, for him to live to see great-grandchildren. Over time, Grandpa admitted that his faith not only returned to him, but that God had become a frequent conversation partner of my grandfather's as Grandpa saw and gave thanks for the many ways in which he felt blessed. The human experience is to live constantly at the intersection of blessing and curse, and it is the person of faith who seeks to understand God's relationship to the good and the bad.

In Exodus, we read of a God who redeems, and in Deuteronomy we learn that God is not only righteous and fair, but also a God of faith. Certainly, we understand human faith in God, but what does it mean that God too can be faithful? I think that just as my grandfather's faith in a God who is just and righteous returned to him in his later years before his death, so too do I believe that God's faith in humanity returned in small part through the life of Wolf Gruca, and through the lives of individual families around the world. Though it is only eight decades since the end of the Shoah, look at how successfully the Jewish people have responded in their abundant pursuit of justice and in their passionate practice of righteousness.

In the Ten Commandments, we read of the sacred obligation to honor one's father and mother. The two tablets of law were seemingly laid out so that on one tablet were written laws regulating the relationship between God and the Israelites. On the other tablet were written laws regulating the behavior among the Israelites. However, Rabbi Moshe ben Nachman (Nachmanides) points out the seeming incongruity in the first tablet containing the law to honor one's father and mother. In explanation, he teaches that how we honor our parents parallels how we honor God. Over the last several decades, the children of Wolf Gruca stepped up to provide for him the way he provided for them for so many years. When children care for their aging parents, God's faith in humanity is restored. My mother—and by extension, my father—did more for Grandpa than any human could reasonably be expected to do for another. When Grandpa said that my mother appeared to him with the face of his mother—though even as Grandpa remarked, my mom is much thinner than she was—I think that it was Grandpa's way of recognizing and thanking my mother for a love that transcended more than just a typical daughter's love for her father. My mom honored him to the extreme and provided for his every want and need. Whatever joy and dignity Grandpa experienced as an old man is because of my mother's love and her untiring care of him. My uncle and aunts were each there in their own way for Grandpa. And the subsequent generations followed suit, though sometimes we all laugh that possibly Grandpa loved his granddaughters-in-law, Rebecca and Brittany, even more than he loved my brother David and me.

In Psalm 27 we read, "Though my father and mother abandon me, the ETERNAL will take me in." For the victims of the Holocaust, it was not only their parents who "abandoned" them (not by choice, obviously), but seemingly God abandoned them as well. It is the children of the survivors, however, and their grandchildren who stepped up to care for these survivors when no one else was left to do so.

"God is faithful," Deuteronomy teaches. Just as God's faith in humanity was restored by watching the children of Wolf Gruca care for him, so too do I believe that God's faith is restored by the way the great-grandchildren of Wolf Gruca and other survivors are devoted to moral and religious living. I know that it brought incredible joy to Grandpa to watch my kids lead prayers in the synagogue and at home at the Sabbath and holiday table, and how, because of my wife, Rebecca's, modeling of intergenerational love, they made their weekly "Shabbat shalom" phone calls to Zayde each Friday afternoon. And I know what incredible joy my grandfather the Holocaust survivor experienced in standing next to Caleb, one of his great-grandsons, as we celebrated Caleb becoming bar mitzvah. Grandpa's presence will be acutely missed in celebrating the coming-of-age ceremonies for his other great-grandchildren.

I know too that God's faith was restored by the efforts to which my brother and my sister-in-law went to bring into this world another great-grandchild for Zayde—to produce yet another descendent of a Holocaust survivor—and the extent to which our grandfather was overjoyed by the birth of his first great-granddaughter Eliana: the one for whom so many prayed and God answered our prayers.

God is faithful. I know that God's faith in humanity was restored by the tremendous love and respect that the synagogue to which we belong offered to this Holocaust survivor and grandfather of their rabbi . . . and how all synagogues honor the survivors in their midst. My family and I are forever grateful for the kindness shown toward him and for the times our community allowed him and me to share his story of survival.

God is faithful. Just as Grandpa found renewed faith throughout his life, I pray that God's faith in humanity is renewed because of the acts of Wolf Gruca's children, grandchildren, and great-grandchildren, along with the communities in which they choose to live and to serve. Indeed, I pray that God's faith in humanity can be restored because of our own commitment to pursuing justice and offering compassion, to practicing righteousness, to strengthening religious practice, and to protecting the right of the State of Israel to exist in safety and security as a Jewish state. Though as humans we struggle to understand how a benevolent and omnipotent God could seemingly fail to act during the Holocaust, we likewise find incredible blessings in our daily lives in the twenty-first century and we see profound miracle as well in the existence of the modern State of Israel.

Biblical Theology #3: God Causes Suffering but Humans Cannot Understand Why

In addition to God rewarding and punishing and the notion of the suffering servant, the biblical book of Job adds yet another theology of suffering that is more comforting in some ways and less comforting in others.

By all accounts, Job is a righteous person who loses everything: his house, his livelihood, his wife, and his children. God then welcomes Job into a conversation wherein Job challenges God much like Abraham did in Genesis; after all, we humans presume God to act at all times with our human sense of justice. In one of the most troubling and yet also beautiful passages of the Hebrew Bible, God explains to Job none-too-gently how *chutzpadik* it is to presume that we humans can understand God's way. In Job we see a continuing theology of God causing suffering, but the story alleviates the burden of trying to understand suffering as a punishment or a message because God reminds us that there are limits to human understanding. With Job, we hear from God the age-old parental message: "Perhaps when you are older, you will understand."

In the midst of suffering, then, the Hebrew Bible offers three entirely different theologies to explain suffering within the human condition: (1) suffering as a punishment or message sent by God against the one or ones suffering; (2) suffering as a message communicated to the non-sufferers through the suffering of innocents; and (3) suffering as sent by God but whose meaning defies human comprehension. All three biblical theologies might suggest, for example, that God indeed placed COVID-19 among us, but leaves room for argument as to why. Would you agree? Did God "cause" the pandemic? What about the Holocaust or other forms of suffering? More to the point, if God parted the Red Sea in biblical times among so many other miracles, where has God been during all the painful moments of the last two thousand years?

4

The Hidden Hand of God

MANY OF US ARE familiar with God's seeming silence. Of the biblical Job we read, "I cry to you, and you do not answer me; I stand, and you [barely] notice me" (Job 30:20). Likewise does King David lament, "My God, my God, why have you forsaken me? Why are you so far from saving me, from the words of my groaning? O my God, I cry by day, but you do not answer, and by night, I get nothing but silence" (Ps 22:1–2). When we are taught that God rewards the righteous and punishes the wicked, but we perceive ourselves to be—if not righteous—than at least not evil, then when God does not answer our prayers with a resounding "Yes!" our faith is called into question. People who pray expecting divine intervention, but whose prayers remain (seemingly) unanswered, wonder why God has forsaken them.

As an indication of how hard life was for Jews in diaspora, the story is told of the sage Rav who once quipped something to the effect of "anyone whose prayers are invariably answered must be a Gentile!"[1] In the times of our sages—much like a significant portion of Jewish history—life was difficult for the Jews; somehow,

1. b. Hag. 5a.

someway, God's "chosen people" suffered while others succeeded. Some of the early rabbis understood their terrible lot to be the result of God hiding God's face. Rav bases his lament on a prophecy from the Torah in which after Moses's death, the Israelites will cease their monotheism. God then reveals to Moses the Israelites' punishment: "On that day my anger will flare up against them; I will forsake them and hide my face from them" (Deut 31:17). Imagine the terrible pain that Rav, his student Rabbi Bardela son of Tavyumei who quotes him, and others must have felt to bemoan their lives so. How they must have suffered to believe that anyone who seemingly had his prayers regularly answered could not be a Jew! The world is full of sadness and suffering.

This Too for Good?

While the Bible offers three theologies of suffering, the generations of murder, persecution, and oppression experienced by the Jews have added to our options for understanding God's seeming silence in the face of tragedy or God's rejection of our prayers. Those who believe that God remains omnipotent and is the one whispering to every blade of grass to grow demonstrate the Jewish concept of *bitachon*: trust. *Bitachon* is the acceptance that everything happens according to God's will, even if that will is in opposition to our own human desires. Moreover, *bitachon* asks that the believer not only accept something as God's will, but to believe that, in God's benevolence, what occurs is for the greater good.

The rabbis relate a story about a certain man named Nachum, who developed the nickname "*Ish Gamzu*," or "The Man of 'This Too.'"[2] Apparently Nachum became famous for the saying "*gam zu l'tovah*: this too is for the good." The Jewish community appointed him to bring a tribute to the emperor. Stopping for the night at a particular inn, the townies raided Nachum's tribute, stealing jewels and pearls and replacing the objects with dirt. Certainly, one might assume that, upon discovering what happened, Nachum would

2. b. Ta'an 21a.

break into a panic: his community's wealth had been stolen and he must choose either to appear before the emperor empty-handed or to return to his people empty-handed. How did Nachum respond? "*Gam zu l'tovah*: this too is for the good." Nachum possessed such strong faith that he believed that whatever happened was the benevolent will of God.

Nachum continued his journey to visit the emperor. When the ruler peered into the treasure chest and saw only earth, the king desired to annihilate the Jewish community for mocking him. How did Nachum respond? "*Gam zu l'tovah*: this too is for the good."

Lo and behold, the miracle worker Elijah the Prophet mystically appeared, dressed secretly before the king as a minister of the court. In this role, Elijah advised the emperor that perhaps the earth in the treasure chest belonged to none other than the patriarch Abraham. Elijah related a story that whenever Abraham would cast the earth into the wind, it transformed into swords and arrows to wield against his enemy.

The emperor put this advice to the test. At the next opportunity, the Emperor's soldiers threw the earth from the chest into the air and, in so doing, helped the Romans to defeat a particular province that had challenged them. Upon this success, the emperor instructed that the treasure chest be filled with precious jewels and pearls and that Nachum should depart for home with these spoils and with great honor. It turned out that, as far as Nachum was concerned, "*gam zu l'tovah*: this too is for the good."

On his journey back home, Nachum returned to the very same inn at which he stayed on the way to see the ruler. Confused because Nachum was not only alive but seemingly enriched, the townies asked Nachum how he had attained such honor before the king. Nachum replied, "I merely gave to the Emperor that which I had brought with me." Sure enough, the townies concluded that the earth with which they had earlier filled the chest after robbing Nachum must be miraculous. They tore down the inn, packaged up the earth, and carried it all the way to the emperor to offer it to him as a gift. After some time, the ruler tested the earth in battle just as he had done with Nachum Ish Gamzu. This time, however, no miracle occurred. The emperor sentenced all the residents of the town to death.

Nachum was a man of deep faith. When one believes that God is acting daily in our lives and that all of God's actions are benevolent, then even when that for which one prays fails to occur or when one suffers, one chooses to believe that such a path is God's will. *Bitachon*—trust in our Creator's choices—is a profound source of comfort and explanation. Like young children in our parents' arms, there is a certain degree of blessed abdication in this approach: If God is in control, then we do not have to be. Everything that occurs, even in the worst possible of situations, "*gam zu l'tovah*: this too is for the good."

A Challenge to Faith

To me, the language of God as a benevolent, omnipotent activist Parent is beautiful and the thought is ideal, but the theology put forth is highly problematic. "The ETERNAL watches over all who love God, but all the wicked God will destroy" (Ps 145:20). "The ETERNAL supports all who stumble and raises all who are bent" (Ps 145:14). What about people who continue to suffer: the child starving in the street or the older adult battling cancer? Does their suffering indicate that God is not responding to their call? And, if God is not responding to their call, does that mean that God considers them evil? Or perhaps that God is simply choosing to ignore them? That even when pain and suffering result, that path is the best? "Where is your God now?" I have heard more than once while sitting alongside the teenager suffering from cancer or standing with the parent desperate for his or her child to recover from a terrible injury.

Does God provide for and heal individuals every day? I am reminded of the movie comedy *Bruce Almighty*, in which the character Bruce (played by Jim Carrey) takes over for God (played by Morgan Freeman) so that he, Bruce, can begin to understand just how difficult God's "job" is. The prayers of the world appear in Bruce's email inbox and, despite the fact that Bruce is able to type at, well, God-speed, he simply cannot keep up with the requests of the faithful. Finally, exhausted from the efforts, Bruce simply replies "yes" to all, fulfilling each person's prayers. The world then essentially comes to a halt, because sometimes people's prayers compete with each other and a "yes" answer to all prayers might be great for individuals but challenging for the world order.

I remember a particular professor at my seminary who taught us documentary hypothesis: that the Bible is a human document written by different individuals. At the same time, I know that he worshiped at a more conservative (and Conservative) synagogue. I scheduled a meeting with him to try to understand how, on the one hand, he could dismiss the divinity of the Bible while, on the other hand, lead a more observant religious life.

The professor took a deep breath and looked me in the eyes. "Aaron, imagine that throughout your whole relationship Rebecca told you that, as a child, she was a world-class figure skater. Then, one day, you found out that not only was she not a world-class figure skater, she had never even put on skates."

I responded to his supposition: "I would be angry at her for lying to me."

"Now," the professor continued, "imagine not that Rebecca told you that she was a world-class figure skater, but that when she was little she always wished she were a world-class figure skater. Rather than being angry and feeling deceived, you might love Rebecca even more because she opened for you a window into her soul. That is what the Bible is," the professor taught me. "Not word-for-word history: the Bible is a window into our ancestors' souls."

In this way, I believe that the Hebrew Bible offers us "memory" in place of "history." I believe that our sacred Scripture offers the world our story: our narrative. With that in mind, and with my experience as the grandchild of Holocaust survivors, I began to approach my theology and scriptural interpretation differently; I needed a non-fundamentalist lens that could allow me to see differently and to understand anew the natural phenomena as far ranging as earthquakes and pandemic viruses, as well as the evil that humans inflict on each other

I learned of a story of an imagined conversation that took place between pagan Romans and the rabbinic sages then living in Rome.[3] The rabbis imagined the gentiles asking, "If God hates idolatry, and God is powerful, why wouldn't God just destroy every idol?" That is to say, if the action God hates the most is idolatry and God is all-powerful, then why would God not just miraculously remove idol worship? The rabbinic sages responded to the pagans, "If people only worshiped statues, then surely God would simply eliminate them! But people worship the sun and the moon, the stars, and the constellations. God cannot destroy those aspects of creation!" Then the rabbis add, "Should God destroy the entire world because of fools?" God cannot destroy the sun, moon, and stars because life on earth requires these aspects of creation even though pagans worshipped them instead of God. "Rather," the sages responded to the pagans, "the world behaves the way it behaves."

Here the sages argue that, in a post-biblical world, God chooses not to suspend the laws of nature and, instead, allows the world to follow its course. Jewish mystics refer to God retreating from direct, overt involvement in the world as *tzimtzum*: God "contracts" or "minimizes" God's self in order to allow for free will. In so doing, God established the laws of the natural world, and so the world and its natural laws exist as they exist. That which happens on a day-to-day level is not of God's direct, intentional doing. Rather, the experience of humanity is the combination of the laws of the natural world intertwined with the consequences of human autonomy.

Whereas God might have been involved in daily human life in the biblical era, as time progressed from the biblical era to the post-biblical era, God withdrew. God stepped back. Like a mother who realizes that she needs to let her children go in order to grow, so too at the end of the biblical era did God recede from direct involvement in earthly affairs.

3. b. ʿAbod. Zar. 54b.

If God Won't Act, We Must

In Psalm 37:5, a verse quoted in the Jewish grace after the meal, the psalmist writes, "I have been young and am now old, but I have never seen a righteous person abandoned, or his children seeking bread." The implications of this verse seem to be that if an adult is lacking in his most basic of needs or is battling a health crisis, or if one's children are experiencing starvation and malnutrition, then that person cannot be righteous. Rabbi Jonathan Sacks of blessed memory quotes his friend Mo Feuerstein (who may have been paraphrasing Rabbi Joseph Soloveitchik) in explaining this complicated verse. "'To see' here means 'to stand still and watch.' The verse thus should be translated, 'I was young and now am old, but I never merely *stood still and watched* while the righteous was forsaken or his children begged for bread.'"[4] That is to say, through this creative reading, we are reminded that when we see suffering, we humans are to follow the lead of our Heavenly Parent by caring for those in need.

For centuries, the scroll of Esther has spoken particularly loudly to the long-oppressed Jewish communities of the diaspora: people who knew from suffering. The story concludes with the Jews not only thwarting the efforts of a Jew-hating government leader, but also with the Jewish people empowered to respond with force to the anti-Semites who threaten them. Yet, nowhere is God mentioned in the entire scroll and, while Jewish tradition accepts that God played a role in the Persian Jews' survival, God's role is conceived as hidden, as behind-the-scenes, as if God were the Parent of adult children supporting our ancestors from afar. In fact, the name "Esther" comes from the Hebrew word for "hidden" because God seemingly disappeared from history.

In the scroll of Esther, as has happened throughout Jewish history, a benign ruler (Ahaseuros) is led astray by the ego of his advisor (Haman) and the Jews bear the brunt of the advisor's hubris and the king's disinterest in protecting the "other" in his

---

4. Sacks, *To Heal*, 57–58.

kingdom. Yet Esther, as a hidden Jew and as queen in Ahaseuros's court, is in the right place at the right time.

By the fourth chapter of the scroll, Esther's uncle Mordecai has learned of Haman's evil plan and seeks to impress upon Esther that she is in a unique position to rescue her people. Mordecai then sent this message to the Queen: "Do not imagine that you, of all the Jews, will escape with your life by being in the king's palace. On the contrary, if you keep silent in this crisis, relief and deliverance will come to the Jews from another quarter, while you and your father's house will perish. And who knows, perhaps you have attained to royal position for just such a crisis" (Esth 4:13–14).

Interestingly, Mordecai is an optimist. In his faith, in his *bitachon*, Mordecai knows that "relief and deliverance will come." Nevertheless, he implores his niece to act: to utilize the power she has attained for the sake of her people. Esther accepts Mordecai's encouragement, puts her life on the line by approaching the king, and persuades her husband to permit the Jews to defend themselves. Neither Mordecai nor Esther put their faith in miracles. Neither Mordecai nor Esther accepted their fate with the words *"gam zu l'tovah."* Instead, even when the die was cast against them (pun intended), they acted. God's presence in the world was seemingly removed; God's hand was hidden. With God stepping back from active duty, then, we are left to look for the signs of God's presence and for what God as our Heavenly Parent wants us to do.

Looking for Signs

The human brain is uniquely equipped to see and to interpret a wide variety of signs. Many of us associate particular occurrences with messages from loved ones reaching out to us from the hereafter: I've been told about chachkas moving on a shelf, certain birds appearing at just the right moment, and other unusual circumstances indicating an other-worldly presence in our vicinity.

Some signs trigger emotions, with certain images serving as signs for our brain to relax or to tense up. Case in point: one summer, my wife, Rebecca, and I took a ten-day "adventure" in which

The Hidden Hand of God

we drove our children from Detroit, through the rough roads of Ohio, and into the mountains of Pennsylvania and upstate New York all the way to the kids' summer camp in Cheshire, Connecticut. To accomplish our mission, we loaded the four of us into our 5.3 liter, V8, 2020 GMC Sierra 1500 pickup truck and attached it to a twenty-eight-foot-long, eleven-foot-high travel trailer camper that miraculously serves simultaneously as both sail and anchor while traveling up and down the various storm-drenched mountain ranges that tower into the sky from Pennsylvania and to the Northeast. The name of our camper? "The Wandering Jew."

Speaking of the signs that evoke emotions, repeatedly Rebecca looked out onto the grand vistas filled with cliffs and trees, and these signs of nature's wide-open expanses caused her to exhale and to feel the sense of freedom and openness she had been needing since the pandemic shrank our world. Me? Those same signs evoked in me a sense of panic and the fight or flight response of man against nature. I tend to most feel freedom and openness when I see signs that read, "Grocery store, next exit" or "CVS 24-hour" or, better yet, "Holiday Inn." Hey, I'm from the suburbs, and these signs make me happy.

In addition to these signs, sometimes we see signs that tell us exactly what to do and when to do it: "speed limit 65" or "caution: dangerous mountain curves ahead." As the driver of this six-ton vehicle combination, I am grateful for explicit signs. In life in general, when each of us is in our own driver's seat, we are often grateful when the signs of how to proceed are blatantly obvious. Usually, however, life's signs are much vaguer and sometimes—sometimes—the signs even contradict each other.

Near the end of the Israelites' journey from Egypt to Israel, most of the generation of the Exodus has passed away, including Miriam the Prophetess and Aaron the High Priest. Moses, knowing that his own demise is likewise imminent, asks God to appoint a successor to lead the Israelite nation in its efforts to reconquer the promised land. God agrees and names Joshua Bin Nun (Joshua, son of Nun) to take over leadership. Though Joshua proved a worthy successor to Moses, God makes clear that Joshua would not engage in the same type of direct relationship with God that Moses knew. Instead, when Joshua wondered whether to move the people forward or to keep them in place, whether to go to war or to hold steady, Joshua is instructed to consult Aaron's son and successor, Elazar, who, as high priest, wears on his breastplate the prophetic Urim and Thumim: signs, symbols, indicators of what Joshua should do (Num 27). Lacking the ability to hear the unmediated word of God, Joshua and Elazar were to ask their questions and look to the Urim and Thumim, and then interpret the messages communicated by the Urim and Thumim in order to decide on their next steps.

Imagine if we too had the ability to consult the mystical Urim and Thumim to determine our direction and to help us as we plan for next steps. I think about the high school senior, trying to determine which college is best for his future. I think about the college graduate poring over numerous job-offers to determine which is best for her. I think too about when we guide ourselves or our loved ones along the health-care journey, and the countless decisions small and large we must make to seek healing and renewal or to begin to let go. Among the greatest questions of our amazing, advanced health-care system is the balance of quantity of life against quality of life: when to make decisions that prolong our time on earth but compromise the experience of living, and when to prioritize the way that we want to live over the length of time to do it. But God no longer speaks directly to humans. And God no longer even communicates to us through Urim and Thumim. Rarely in life and especially in our most difficult of decisions do the signs all point in the same direction.

Already by the time of the later Israelite kings, when the rulers were trying to decide whether to lead their people to war, they were required to consult with the Sanhedrin: the collection of seventy-one rabbinic elders who would guide the kings' decisions.[5] Even the Israelite kings needed their congress's approval to go to war, and, if you think getting politicians in DC to agree on anything is tough, try putting a group of seventy-one rabbis in one room and

5. b. Sanh. 16a.

see if they will ever agree. More to the point, we learn that in the absence of clear direction, we are to consult a myriad perspectives and opinions before making the most important decisions in our life. This of course stands in contradistinction to what most of us do. Instead, we might consult a spouse, a parent, or one or two similarly minded friends who will rarely tell us that we are wrong. We certainly know the reality of the echo chambers to be true in the political realm as well, when most of us read the newspapers that already support our beliefs and accept only the opinions of the social media posts and internet articles telling us exactly what we want to hear. Rather, whether it is a matter of politics, or even more important matters like health-care decisions and paths in life, our most important decisions need ample input from a variety of sources and especially those who are impartial. Unlike God did with Moses and Miriam, God isn't speaking to us directly.

On the second day of our trip out east, we were searching for the campsite in western Pennsylvania that we had booked a few weeks prior to departing for our adventure. Sure enough, the GPS told us one direction, but the signs clearly pointed to something else. "Detour ahead," we read five miles from the campsite, "bridge out." The signs said the same again four miles out and three miles. What should we do? Do we follow the GPS, or do we follow the signs?

Not sure what to do, Rebecca went to the website of the campgrounds: ignore the GPS, it told us, and ignore the detour signs too. The website gave us its own set of directions. With a one in three chance of success—including the risk of driving up to an out-of-commission bridge and needing to figure out how to do a three-hundred-point-turn on a narrow road to get the truck and camper turned around—we made our choice. We followed the directions on the campground's website; surely they would know best. As we proceeded, the GPS yelled at us to turn. At the same time, the warning signs at the side of the road about the out-of-commission bridge increased in frequency. "Detour ahead: bridge out." And again, "Detour ahead: bridge out." We continued forward, forward, forward, until about one-hundred yards before the broken bridge . . . we turned comfortably into the campsite. There were no Urim. There were no Thumim. There was not even a Sanhedrin with whom to consult. So we put our trust in a website and our faith in God and, thanks be, we arrived safely. We relied on the correct signs.

The human brain is uniquely equipped to see and to interpret a wide variety of signs. Sometimes the signs ignite our brain and sometimes the signs inspire our emotions. In addition to signs from the great beyond and signs that trigger our feelings, sometimes we see signs that tell us exactly what to do. Usually, however, life's signs are much vaguer and sometimes—sometimes—the signs even contradict each other. In this ever more complex world in which we are flooded with information and overwhelmed by opinions, a world in which God's hands are hidden, we are obligated like the Israelite kings before us to consult a wide breadth of experts before making the best decisions that we can make for ourselves and for our loved ones. As adult children of our Heavenly Parent, decisions are ours to make.

"The world behaves the way the world behaves," the Talmud explains. Like the empty-nester Parent, God is available for comfort, support, and yes, advice. But when something needs to be done, we do not wait for God to step in. We step up.

God Wants Us to Lead a Meaningful Life

5

Learning from God to Become Adults

PERHAPS, THEN, A FULLER way to understand God as our Heavenly Parent is to perceive ourselves as adult children and God as our empty-nester Parent. The parent of an adult continues to love his or her child and continues to serve as a resource for support and, at times, for sustenance too. But the adult child realizes that his or her parents cannot solve every problem. As adults, we know that even though our parents may have some extra money and even though our parents may have room in their house and food in their refrigerator, we have a responsibility to take care of ourselves independent of their resources. In a healthy relationship between parents and adult children, the emotional support continues forever, but the material assistance along with the notion that a parent can solve all problems are eliminated.

Following God's Lead

Already by the end of the five books of Moses, God begins to nudge the Israelites out of the nest. For forty years, God provided everything for them night and day. From food to water to shelter to protection to ensuring their clothes never wore out, God took care of everything. But then, in Deuteronomy, Moses begins preparing the Israelites for life without his leadership and without God providing for their every need. I am reminded of when, in my senior year of high school, my mother began teaching me to cook and to do laundry: her recipes became my recipes; her washing technique became my washing technique. If one is on his own, one needs to take care of one's self, and what better lead to follow than that of a loving parent!

So it is that in Deuteronomy 13:5, Moses instructs the Israelites, "After the ETERNAL your God you shall walk." Yet isn't it seemingly nonsensical that a human could "walk" like God? Rather, we learn subsequently that just as God clothed the naked, so too must we provide financial support for the indigent. Just as God visited the sick and consoled mourners, so too must we provide emotional support for those who are in need. And just as God buried the dead, so too must we care even for those who cannot repay our kindness.[1]

God is an empty-nester Parent, looking for us, God's children, to step up, to follow her lead, to care for ourselves, and to care for others. In this way, we live the meaningful life that God expects of us.

Living a Meaningful Life

Many years ago, I met with an acquaintance interested in parenting advice. This man, who is about my age, is like me, the grandson of Holocaust survivors. He strongly identifies as a Jew, and he told me that, though not religious, he likes being Jewish. Then things became more complicated. His wife, he told me, identifies strongly as Catholic, though she only practices occasionally. Their marriage hummed along with no religious problems at all until, of course, a child came along. To not pick a side, they decided to raise the child without any religion. This man came to seek my advice on how to

1. b. Sotah 14a.

raise a mensch—a good human being—without any of the formal structures of religion like holidays, rituals, prayer, or community. He wanted to know the secrets of four thousand years of Jewish life, this man told me, but he only wanted to know the "essence" of being Jewish: not all that "other stuff."

I collected my thoughts for a moment. The prophets and sages all weighed in on that very question: what is the essence of being Jewish? And I thought carefully about the answers offered by those prophets and sages. "Do justice, love kindness, walk humbly with God," the prophet Micah taught (Mic 6:8). "Do not do unto others as you would not want done unto you," taught the sage Hillel.[2] And then I thought about the question this man was asking me regarding twenty-first-century parenting. He came seeking the core of it all: not Judaism's most important teaching, but its collective wisdom.

Gratitude, Obligation, and Joy

As I processed his question about the essence of Judaism, I walked over to my desk; I opened my drawer, removed a pad of paper, and wrote down a math equation: gratitude + obligation + joy = the essence of Judaism. Then I added, gratitude + obligation + joy = the meaning of life. The man thought about it for a moment. "Gratitude plus obligation plus joy," he repeated.

"That's right," I told him. "Our prayer services are filled with poems and prose that express gratitude for every aspect of our lives: from simply being able to wake up in the morning all the way to the promise of redemption. From waking up, to eating, to going to the bathroom, and so much more, we are taught to recite prayers of thanksgiving each day, 7 days a week, 365 days a year." That's expressing gratitude.

"But we cannot simply be grateful," I told him. "God has expectations of us. The biblical commandments are what God expects of us in order to deepen our relationship with our Heavenly

2. b. Šabb. 31a.

Parent, and God wants us to strive to make this world a better place. And commandments are more than just 'good deeds,'" I told the man. "If you're tired, you can take a break from good deeds. But commandments: those we do whether we want to or not. Prayers are how we show our appreciation for all that we have, but commandments are how we emulate our Heavenly Parent by giving to and doing for others. Gratitude plus obligation."

"And I get the 'joy' piece," my acquaintance chimed in. "Jewish living is joyful living. There's a lot of fun there," he reminded himself more than me. Together we spoke of his happy memories of holiday celebrations in the home, his bar mitzvah service at the synagogue, and the feelings that come from being part of a community and a people. Gratitude + obligation + joy: the essence of Judaism and the meaning of life.

For Jews, this meaning of life is infused throughout our holiest season. In the book of Numbers (29), the holidays that we today call Rosh Hashanah, Yom Kippur, and Sukkot are listed back-to-back-to-back.[3] It's no coincidence. For our ancestor farmers living in an agrarian society, autumn was indeed a season of judgment. It was at this time of year that our ancestors learned whether they could harvest enough food to last through the winter. It was at this time of year that they would pray for an ample rainy season—not too much rain and not too little—so that the spring would yield its fruit to sustain them through the dry summer. For our ancestors, Rosh Hashanah, Yom Kippur, and Sukkot combined to make a season of judgment, and also a season of gratitude, an understanding of their sense of obligation, and even of joy. After all, life is about learning to find happiness in the midst of our fragility.

In our own day, Jews continue to celebrate the big three autumn holidays. For us, Rosh Hashanah is a day infused with celebration—reflection as well, for sure, on the role of God's hidden hand in our lives—but with a sense of joy, hope, and promise. We

3. In the Bible, these sacred occasions are referred to as the first day of the seventh month (Rosh Hashanah, the Jewish New Year), the tenth day of the seventh month (Yom Kippur, the Jewish Day of Atonement), and the fifteenth day of the seventh month (Sukkot, the Festival of Booths).

gather with friends and family for lunch or dinners. Our prayer melodies are often triumphant. And, hoping that we are blessed with another year of health and life, we give thanks for the year that was. Rosh Hashanah is a time of gratitude for all the blessings in our lives.

Then we come to Yom Kippur. Though we are in the twenty-first century, the Day of Atonement has not lost its significance as a day in which we reflect on our achievements and failures, our mortality, and our opportunity to still make changes in our lives. On Yom Kippur we consider the obligations God has set upon us—the *mitzvot*—and we pound our chest in sadness at knowing that too often we missed the mark. Of course, it is easy to spend Yom Kippur focusing on ourselves: our own goals and desires. It is for this reason that the rabbis selected for the prophetic reading of Yom Kippur (what's called the *haftarah*) the words of God as found in the book of Isaiah. The prophet recounts how the Israelites reached out to God daily, studied Torah, and fasted in repentance. Yet, despite these righteous behaviors, they complained that they still did not feel God's presence.

Then, like the parent whose adult children have gone astray, God chastises our ancestors for their insolence. "Do you call this a fast? . . . No," God bellows. "No, this is the fast I desire: to unlock the fetters of wickedness and untie the cords of the yoke; to let the oppressed go free. . . . It is to share your bread with the hungry, and to take the wretched poor into your home. When you see the naked, to clothe them, and do not ignore your own people" (Isa 58:5–7). By linking this text with the Day of Atonement, the rabbis use the teachings of Isaiah to remind us that Yom Kippur is about so much more than fasting and repenting to God. We are hungry for one day. We are tired and in need for one day. Too many in this world, though, hunger every day. Too many are in need every day. And it is our obligation to care for those that we can. If Rosh Hashanah is about gratitude, Yom Kippur is certainly about obligation.

Then, five days after Yom Kippur, we celebrate the holiday of Sukkot, called by the rabbis "The Season of Our Joy." This

Festival of Booths is a family holiday. The fragrance of the lulav (the combination of palm, willow, and myrtle) and the etrog (citron) enliven our senses (Lev 23:40). The Sukkah itself begs us to surround ourselves with family, and the traditions of the holiday encourage us to invite friends to share in celebration. The week of Sukkot concludes with Shemini Atzeret (Num 29:35) with its prayers for rain in Israel and Simchat Torah when we dance with the Torah scrolls—literally, dancing around the synagogue with Torah scrolls. Sukkot is pure joy. Rosh Hashanah + Yom Kippur + Sukkot = gratitude + obligation + joy. This is the essence of Judaism and this is the meaning of life.

As the adult children of God, we possess a great deal of power to control the choices in our lives. Are you happy with the choices you are making? Does the way you live your life truly reflect your priorities? Your values? Is how you are spending your money representative of what is most important to you? Is how you spend your time reflective of that which matters most? And, perhaps just as important, will you do what is "right and good" in the eyes of our Heavenly Parent?

I came across an image of a young boy standing next to his father as the father dressed for work in the morning. It's a scene I'm sure many of us have experienced as we busily get ready for our day while our children keep us company. The boy looks up at his father and says, "Dad, how much money do you make per hour?" The father, surprised by his young son's question but proud of his wages responds, "Oh, about $50 per hour. Why do you ask?" The little boy looks back up at his father and responds, "Daddy, if I have $50 in my piggy bank, will you spend an hour with me?" Life is all about the choices we make, how we respond to the situations we face, and the lessons we learn along the way.

Indulge me for a moment if you would. Think about someone in your life who is no longer here: a parent or grandparent, a spouse, a friend. See their face, the lines and the wrinkles around their eyes or their mouth. Look at their hands, perhaps strong, perhaps soft. What would your loved one say to you about how you are living your life? Would they be proud? Disappointed? What advice would they give you? Which direction would they tell you to take?

A month after that initial meeting, I met a second time with the young father who had come to see me. He had clearly given thought to what we had discussed the first time. We had another good conversation. He asked if he could bring his wife back to meet me sometime this fall. "Of course," I told him.

"But rabbi," he said, "we're still not looking to raise our son Jewish."

"I hear you. Just start with the essence of Judaism," I told him, "and let's keep talking."

Gratitude + obligation + joy. It's okay, you can even say it with me: gratitude + obligation + joy. The meaning of life.

Every day we have choices. As Moses says in the Torah, "Choose life that you may live" (Deut 30:19). And as I like to say, choose gratitude. Choose obligation. Choose joy. That is the essence of Judaism, and I believe that is the meaning of life.

An Acronym Worth Remembering

I shared this message about gratitude, obligation, and joy with my congregation. Afterward, someone came up to me, offered a nice compliment, and then made a suggestion. "Rabbi," he said, "instead of gratitude, obligation, and joy, it should be gratitude, obligation, and delight."

I thought about that for a moment. "But I like the word joy better than delight," I informed the man.

"Yes, Rabbi," he responded. "But gratitude, obligation, and delight make for a far better acronym." I looked at the man while I contemplated his suggestion. Gratitude; obligation; delight? Gratitude. Obligation. Delight: G.O.D.

6

Gratitude

IN MY MIND, THERE is no question that gratitude is at the heart of living a life of meaning. I believe too that among the characteristics that God most wants for us, God's adult children, is to be grateful. This is, after all, the second message behind the first commandment: "I am the ETERNAL your God who brought you out of the land of Egypt, the house of bondage." Unfortunately for most, however, gratitude hardly comes easy and that is because humility lies at the foundation of gratitude. Humility is a trait lacking far too much in the twenty-first century.

On Humility

Humility precedes gratitude, and humility and gratitude are the building blocks upon which our relationship with God is formed.

Interestingly, juxtaposed with the Israelites' encounter with God at Sinai, Moses's father-in-law Jethro, along with Moses's wife Tziporah and their two children, reunite with the Israelite shepherd-prince who just led the Israelites out of Egypt. Jethro has heard of the miraculous events of the day; nevertheless, he allows his son-in-law to share the stories in his own words.

"Jethro, priest of Midian, Moses's father-in-law, heard all that God had done for Moses and for Israel, God's people, how the ETERNAL had brought Israel out from Egypt," Exodus 18:1 tells us. It continues seven verses later, "Moses then recounted to his father-in-law everything that the ETERNAL had done to Pharaoh and to the Egyptians for Israel's sake, all the hardships that had befallen them on the way, and how the ETERNAL had delivered them." Jethro had heard the stories already and yet allowed Moses nevertheless to recount them.

Indeed, listening to stories that you have heard before is humility. When we allow our spouses or our children or our parents and grandparents the opportunity to repeat stories about which they are excited, we honor them. There is profound respect and compassion in this act of humility; when we listen deeply and fully, we grant dignity to the speaker. We also just might learn something that we missed in a previous telling.

Moses and his father-in-law Jethro's conversation is two-ways, however: just as Jethro listens to Moses, Moses listens to Jethro. "The next day, Moses sat to adjudicate among the people. The people then stood over Moses from morning until evening. When Moses's father-in-law observed how much he was doing for the people, [Jethro] said, 'What is this thing that you are doing for the people? Why do you sit alone, while all the people stand above you from morning until evening?'" (Exod 18:13–14).

Jethro is stunned by the burden Moses is carrying. Jethro the Midianite priest, himself a strong leader, laid out a plan for Moses to appoint judges who might take on the lesser cases so that the entire nation could be served more efficiently and judiciously. For the system to work, Moses needed to accept and to trust the judges' rulings.

Moses—former prince of Egypt and the man appointed to redeem the Israelites from exile, to receive God's Law, and to lead the Israelites to the promised land—heeded his father-in-law's advice. For Moses to listen to the wisdom of another person, let alone a person of a significantly different background than his own, demonstrates Moses's profound humility. Moreover, as the story continues, we see that Moses carries out Jethro's plan and, in so doing, Moses further shows his humility in allowing others to lead: the judges mentioned in this portion; Aaron and Miriam; and later, Joshua.

While Moses and Jethro succeed because of their humility, their ancestors demonstrate how humility can be a struggle. In Genesis, we read of Isaac's favoritism toward Esau and Rebecca's favoritism toward Esau's twin brother, Jacob. We learn also that Esau, who was born seconds before his brother and thus merited all the rights in the ancient world ascribed to the firstborn, was willing to trade his birthright to Jacob for a cup of lentil soup. Additionally, we learn that Rebecca and Jacob duped their blind husband and father Isaac into further affirming this transference of primogeniture when he, Isaac, unknowingly conferred the first-born's blessing onto Jacob.

Esau quickly finds out about Jacob's trickery. As such, Jacob flees for his life from his brother, Esau, and their mother, Rebecca, directs Jacob to travel outside the land of Israel toward her birth-place: in part for safety, but also to find a wife among her kin. There in his mother's hometown of Haran, Jacob the trickster becomes Jacob the tricked, when father-in-law-to-be Laban (Rebecca's brother and thus Jacob's uncle) swaps under the wedding canopy older sister Leah for Jacob's love, the younger sister Rachel.

That experience humbled the patriarch. Jacob returns twenty years later to the promised land as a more mature, thoughtful man. He has become a husband, father, and in possession of great wealth. Jacob knows that, in returning to the place of his birth, he must encounter his big brother. Will Esau embrace Jacob after so many years apart, or will Esau seek vengeance against the brother who seemingly stole so much from him?

Immediately before entering what will later become known as the land of Israel, Jacob bows low in prayer, whispering to our Creator: "I am unworthy of all the kindness and the truth that you have so steadfastly shown your servant" (Gen 32:11). The English "I am unworthy" is a translation of the Hebrew word *katonti*: an unusual but beautiful verb, deriving from the root *katan*, small. Jacob quite literally shrinks himself before God. Jacob humbles himself before the Ruler of rulers, our Heavenly Sovereign and Parent.

Then Jacob prays, "Save me, please, from the hand of my brother, from the hand of Esau" (Gen 32:12). Jacob offers humility first and petition second. Jacob is fully aware how unworthy he is of God's unending love. Nevertheless, in making requests from God, Jacob relies on God's kindness and forgiveness. Jacob the trickster then became Jacob the tricked. Then Jacob the tricked grows up and discovers that humility is the secret foundational building block of a life of meaning.

Fast forward again, and Jacob is an old man; his children are grown. Jacob's life has not been an easy one. His favorite son, Joseph (yes, Jacob played favorites just as his parents did), was lost with Jacob believing that Joseph had been killed by a wild animal. Jacob's daughter, Dinah, is assaulted and Jacob's children rise to avenge their sister. In so doing, they placed themselves on shaky moral ground and risked furthering warfare with their neighbors. After all that, a terrible famine descends upon Israel and Jacob and his family are threatened. The silver lining, of course, is that all these challenges ultimately bring Jacob back together with his son Joseph.

Notwithstanding the reunification of Jacob and Joseph, the impact of Jacob's life has taken its toll on the patriarch. In fact, when Pharaoh encounters the elder Jacob, he appears astonished by just how old Jacob looks. "How old are you!?" Pharaoh asks (Gen 47:8). Pharaoh is looking upon the face of a man who is withered and broken. "How old *are* you!?" The patriarch responds, "The years of my sojourn [on earth amount to] 130. Few and difficult the years of my life have been, and they do not even come up to the life spans of my fathers during their sojourns" (Gen 47:9). Jacob is a broken man.

Somehow, as he nears the end of his life, Jacob experiences an epiphany and thereby rallies to bequeath to his descendants an incredible inheritance. "The eyes of Israel (i.e., Jacob) were heavy with age," the Torah tells us (Gen 48:10). Our rabbis explain, however, that in this case, old age—*zokein* in Hebrew—is actually a secret acronym for *zeh kanah*: "Jacob had acquired."[1] But what had Jacob acquired?

In the Talmud, the rabbis teach us that Jacob had acquired a particular kind of wisdom: they believed that Jacob studied at a yeshiva and therefore acquired knowledge of Jewish law. I might suggest something in addition, however, because what happens next is incredibly profound. Joseph, Jacob's long-lost son with whom he has become only slightly reacquainted (more on that later), places his sons—Jacob's grandsons—on Jacob's lap. In a wonderfully warm, intimate moment, we hear Jacob say to his son, "I never expected to see you again, and here God has let me see your children as well" (Gen 48:11). In Jacob's final days, the great wisdom he acquired was the blessing of gratitude.

The sages too learned this wisdom about the power of giving thanks and they institutionalized it within Judaism. In fact, there is an entire tractate of the Talmud—Tractate Brachot—devoted nearly exclusively to helping us express our gratitude for the various blessings in our life.

Jewish tradition encourages us to say "thank you" up to one hundred times each day, with specific blessings for food and drink; for observing with any of our senses the miracles of nature, such as a rainbow, thunderstorm, or viewing an ocean; for basic life functions, such as going to the bathroom; and for key moments in our life. The Talmud teaches us to recite these blessings of gratitude in the form *baruch ata*—blessed are you. The word *baruch*—blessed—is connected to the word *birkayim*: knees. When we recite a blessing of thanksgiving, we place ourselves metaphorically on our knees before God: humility, again, being the foundation of gratitude. In fact, the Talmud records Rabbi Hanina Bar Papa teaching, "If one enjoys something from this world without a blessing, it is as if they have stolen from God and from the community of Israel."[2]

---

1. b. Yoma 28b.
2. b. Ber. 35b.

7

Obligation

THE NOTION OF "OBLIGATION" is central to adulthood, and central to acting as an adult child of God. Jewish tradition reveals that the Torah obligates the Jewish people to fulfill 613 commandments, though it "only" obligates non-Jews to fulfill seven commandments (known as the Noahide laws because they were given to the world following the flood of Noah's time). I remember teaching this idea when I served as a guest speaker one particular year in a local public high school's world religions class. A young man, probably age fifteen or sixteen, then raised his hand. "The Jewish people are obligated to 613 commandments?" He was seeking clarity and I answered him in the affirmative. "And non-Jews are subject to seven commandments?" I responded again in the affirmative. Without missing a beat, the young man then interjected, "Looks like someone got the raw end of that deal!"

We all laughed. In truth, though, as Jewish adults we come to realize that fulfilling ritual commandments gives us meaning by deepening our sense of the Divine's presence in our lives, by allowing us to express gratitude for the small blessings in our lives, and by helping us to mark the major moments in our lives. We strive to fulfill the ethical commandments because doing so is the right thing to do; because doing so feels good; and because doing so gives us purpose beyond ourselves. Whether we are Jewish or not, as adults and as faithful human beings, we accept that obligations are a central feature of maturity.

Interestingly, did you know that the adhesive material on the back of Israeli postage stamps is certified kosher? I remember the particular conversion of a unique young man. At age fifteen and well before he ever met a rabbi or sat in a synagogue, sitting in his high school in a very non-Jewish part of suburban Detroit, this young man somehow came across the fact that the adhesive material on the back of Israeli postage stamps is certified kosher. Upon learning this information, the young man asked three questions: What is Israel? What is "kosher"? And why would anyone care about the ingredients of the adhesive material on the back of a postage stamp? These questions started the young adult on a journey of learning and discovery, of spirituality and questioning, that led him several years later to convert to Judaism. In learning one piece of seemingly random information, this young man's life changed forever. Now that's a valuable postage stamp!

For my wife, Rebecca, and me, it took two events in the life cycle to make us change our lives: the death in 2007 of my mother-in-law, Carol—may she rest in peace—and the birth of our son Caleb one month later: Caleb being named for Carol. As the grandchild of ultra-Orthodox Jews on one side and Holocaust survivors on the other, Jewish tradition has always played an important role in my upbringing and my adult life. Rebecca, too, though raised on a sheep farm in Michigan's Upper Peninsula, was steeped in Jewish life from birth, having to cross the international bridge each week to the synagogue in Sault Ste. Marie, Ontario, for Religious School . . . taught by her mother.

Rebecca and I loved Judaism, and we lived a Jewish life. However, with Carol's passing, we realized how short life truly is and so we decided to take another step in our spiritual journey: we became *shomer Shabbat* (Sabbath observant): no television for twenty-five hours each week (twenty-fours of the Sabbath day, and one extra hour to be sure); no driving for an entire day; and most certainly, no cell phones or computers for the entire Sabbath. Moreover, in Caleb's birth, Rebecca and I dedicated ourselves to utilizing Jewish tradition to raise, God-willing, a mensch; to creating a family open to God's miracles in our every-day life; and to embracing through Jewish ritual moments of meaning and awe. Granted, it took Rebecca and me more than a postage stamp to change our lives, but, with some anxiety and much hope, we took that leap of faith. I changed my career path, and we moved across town. We altered our lifestyle and switched communities to find one accommodating of our religious choices. We were and we are on a journey.

Change is a scary thing—especially in the realm of religion. We humans are indeed stubborn and stiff-necked, and we are creatures of habit too, mostly content to live lives of familiarity and sameness. We find comfort in the status quo. However, the inspiration of a postage stamp, the life change after the death of a loved one, or the birth of a child holds no candle to the lifestyle change discussed in the story of Abraham and Sarah.

Seemingly entirely out of the blue Abraham—already an old man—hears a command from above telling him, "Go forth from your land; from the place of your birth; from your father's home," from everything you've come to know and understand about the world, "to a land that I will show you" (Gen 12:1). God does not tell Abraham to which land he will travel nor what will be there waiting for him when he arrives. What does Abraham say? We have no idea. In response to God's declaration to him, all we know is that "then Abraham went." As a reward for our ancestors' journey, God establishes a covenant—a contract—with Abraham and Sarah in which God promises to make their descendants as numerous as the stars in the sky and to give to those descendants the beautiful land we now call Israel.

Judaism, Christianity, and Islam exist today because Abraham was willing to change the life to which he had become accustomed, taking one step after another in his relationship with God. We are here today because Abraham and generations after him were willing to investigate their hearts and to commit themselves ever deeper to God and to religious life.

Despite excellent cell phone coverage, not all of us receive a direct call from God like Abraham did. And not all of us are attune enough to see God in the adhesive material on the back of a postage stamp. For most of us, we need to have handed to us those "a-ha" or "light bulb" moments that inspire us to deepen our commitment to our heritage. For most of us it takes something as sad as the death of a loved one; as miraculous as the birth of a child; or as traumatic as a significant illness to make us work to deepen our relationship with God.

From Faith to Action

Many years ago, I taught an adult education class entitled "The Meaning of Life." One of the texts we explored was the book *The Last Lecture* by Randy Pausch and Jeffrey Zaslow (my co-teacher, now of blessed memory). In Professor Pausch's illness, he reminded his listeners and readers that we must live each and every day as if it were our last: spending as much time with our families as possible; giving other people the benefit of the doubt; showing kindness even in the face of anger; and smiling more. "Never lose your child-like wonder," Pausch reminds us, and help others.[1] "Loyalty is a two-way street."[2] And never give up. It sounds to me like Professor Pausch lived a mindful life to begin with, but it took a diagnosis of pancreatic cancer for him to live each moment to its fullest and to strive each day for a deeper level of holiness and meaning. Sadly, this incredible man required an encounter with mortality to inspire him one more step in his spiritual journey.

Like Professor Randy Pausch, Moses too offered a last lecture. In Moses's last lecture, also known as Deuteronomy, Moses tells us, "Behold, I place before you this day life and goodness, death and wickedness. For I command you this day to love the

---

1. Pausch and Zaslow, *Last Lecture*, 165.
2. Pausch and Zaslow, *Last Lecture*, 153.

ETERNAL your God, to walk in God's ways, and to keep God's commandments" (Deut 30:15–16). And what is the system of walking in God's ways and following the commandments called? *Halachah*. While often translated as "Jewish law," *halachah* actually means walking, journeying, progressing, and taking one small step after another.

An old joke is told of a child who approaches her rabbi.

"I have a question," the child stated.

"What's that?" The rabbi answered.

"Well according to the Bible, the children of Israel crossed the Red Sea, right?"

"Right."

"And the children of Israel beat up the Philistines, right?"

"Er—right."

"And the children of Israel built the Holy Temple, right?"

"Again you're right," the rabbi told her.

"And the children of Israel fought the Egyptians, and the children of Israel fought the Romans, and the children of Israel were always doing something important, right?"

"All that is right, too," the rabbi agreed. "So, what's your question?"

"What I wanna know is this," the young child demanded. "If the children of Israel were busy doing all that, what were the grown-ups doing?"

We expect our children to be full-time students who always strive to better themselves, but what about us adults? Perpetual betterment is one of the central messages of the Jewish holiday of Chanukah too. In the Talmud, scholars from more than 1,500 years ago discuss how to celebrate the even older holiday in which the Maccabees defeated the Greek Syrians to reclaim the Holy Temple of Jerusalem and to reestablish Jewish autonomy over the land of Israel. Recounting the day's supply of menorah oil that miraculously lasted for eight days until new oil could be produced, two competing notions arose as to how to light the chanukiyah: the nine-branched candelabra with which Chanukah is celebrated.

God Wants Us to Lead a Meaningful Life

The school of Shammai proposed that on the first day of the holiday, eight candles should be lit and then each successive night of Chanukah should see one candle removed. This way, as later rabbis come to explain, the celebrants would know what day of the holiday they were marking and how many days remained. Alternatively, other rabbis sought to explain Shammai's ruling by reminding us that Chanukah was really "just" a delayed celebration of the holiday of Sukkot: the Festival of Booths. Because the Greeks had desecrated the Holy Temple the Jews were unable to celebrate Sukkot until two months after the biblically mandated date. Perhaps, then, just as the daily sacrifices were reduced each day of the Sukkot holiday, Shammai was suggesting that the holiday candles should reduce by one each day as well.

However, the school of Hillel disagreed with the school of Shammai. Hillel taught that only one candle should be lit on the first day; two candles lit on the second day, and one candle added each day of the holiday until, on the final night of Chanukah, the entire candelabra is alive with flames. The prevailing theory behind Hillel's teaching is that we should always elevate in matters of holiness. Hillel's practice won, and for centuries Jews celebrate Chanukah by lighting one additional candle each night of the holiday. We always strive to elevate in matters of holiness.[3]

Of course, elevating our holiness is no easy task. We are all busy people. There is work and carpool; there are after-school activities and chores to be done around the house. It is very difficult to change our lifestyles, even to take one more baby step on our spiritual journeys. Yet people have succeeded; it can be done. As we read daily in our car's side mirrors, "objects are closer than they appear." So too is it with God and with leading a life of meaning and purpose: they are closer than they appear. All it takes, though, is one more step.

3. b. Šabb. 21b.

From Adolescence to Adulthood: The Obligation to Act Morally and Righteously

Do you remember when you were seventeen and you believed that, if you really tried hard enough, you could change the world? Do you remember the day your first child was born when you looked into the eyes of that beautiful baby and prayed with all your heart that the world would be a better place when that child grew up? I look around our great nation and I see people so discouraged by discrimination, anti-Semitism, inequality, the financial situation, the seemingly endless political squabbling, the violence, and the wars raging throughout the world that all we want to do is sit in front of our televisions, hold our families, and escape. Now mind you, I'm all for "vegging" out as much as the next guy. I love playing basketball with my kids, going for walks with my beautiful wife, and joining friends for dinner. But frankly, I do not believe that God put us here merely to have fun or simply to be happy, though living joyfully is a central part of our lives. Instead, as God said of Adam and Eve (Gen 2:15), our job on earth is "to work and to protect" the land. But at some point, you must wonder: are we as a society becoming too complacent? Are we becoming too relaxed? Are we merely too content to complain about the world rather than doing something to change it?

But then we come to Gen 22:1: "It was after these things that God tested Abraham." How does he respond? Abraham is no longer the naive boy who wordlessly left his homeland earlier in Genesis and so, this time, we hear Abraham's voice. With one Hebrew word, Abraham responds to God: "*Hineni.*" I picture Abraham standing there, looking up at the heavens and beating his chest: "Here I am, God. Bring it." After all that Abraham had done to serve God and to receive the reward of offspring, God asks of Abraham the unthinkable: "Take now your son, your only son, the one that you love . . . Isaac . . . and offer him up on one of the mountains that I will show you." What kind of a God asks this and what kind of a man accepts such a request?

In Jewish thought, it could only be a God of strength to ask and a man of faith to accept; it could only be a God who trusts the recipient of such a command and a man who trusts his God enough to go through each step of the way, all the while believing that God would never force his hand in this way. The rabbinic sages defend both God and Abraham in this terribly troublesome story of the binding of Isaac by telling us that God would never have asked Abraham to go all the way with the sacrifice; rather, God was showing the world that Abraham was so committed to our Creator that he was willing to do anything for God. Similarly, Abraham trusted God so much that he knew that God would never ask him to commit such a grave action and, in the end, both God and Abraham were right. Abraham passed the test and God committed to fulfilling his promise to Abraham: to make him the father of many nations and to grant to his descendants the land of Israel. And, ultimately, what was God's test of Abraham? To take one step—however scary, however new, however different, and however challenging—to take one more step on his spiritual journey. Jews and Judaism, Christians and Christianity, Muslims and Islam exist today because of Abraham's strength of faith.

Yet God is not speaking to us today as clearly and as powerfully as God spoke to Abraham. Instead, as God's adult children, we must find God's words within us, and we must on our own proclaim, "I will do better. I will try harder. I will make this place better for my children than it is for me. I will restore hope to the world." This is *our* moment to say *hineni*, here I am to answer God's call.

God's adult children set the ethical standard for a world spinning out of control. When people scale back their donations during a recession, God's adult child says, "I will continue to feed the hungry. *Hineni.*" When people believe wrongly that the internet provides sufficient community through social networking sites and email, God's adult child says the computer is not enough. "I have to go out into the world to embrace the mourner; to celebrate with the engaged and the newly married; and to rejoice with those coming of age. I have to go to my house of worship to sit among others and thus be inspired to make my life better. *Hineni.*" And when everything is available to us with the click of the button and a delivery drop-off, God's adult child remembers that life often becomes more meaningful through self-sacrifice. We celebrate that our lives are better, stronger, and holier for our commitment to Sabbath observance, to dietary laws, and to prayer. Like Abraham before us, today we say "*hineni.*"

It all comes down to one word: *hineni.* We say "*hineni*" when we use the rituals and customs of our faith tradition to bring meaning to our lives and to unite us with the community. We say "*hineni*" when we teach the world by example how to care for the poor, the widowed, and the orphan. We say "*hineni*" when we regularly visit the sick or the aged and take care of those with special needs. We say "*hineni*" when we teach the world how to create a fair, just society. We say "*hineni*" when we show the world that religion is a force for good, and we say "*hineni*" when we demonstrate that faith and intellectualism are not contradictory notions. We honor our ancestors, including our parents and grandparents, who were brave enough to say "*hineni,*" and then we look at our lives and ask ourselves how we can do better: in our relationships to God and in our relationships with each other. *Hineni.* Let us speak out and stand up. *Hineni.* Let us turn to community and return to our faith. *Hineni.* Let us say, "We can change the world" because if we do not say it, perhaps no one will. *Hineni.*

The Obligation of Hope

As the adult children of the Holy One, our role is to act in this world by lifting the fallen, by showing kindness even to the undeserving, and by pursuing justice. Our role is also to bring hope.

There is a certain growing hopelessness in our world. Natural disasters. War. Racism. Anti-Semitism. Homophobia. Undocumented immigration. Gun violence. The continued rise of extremism on both sides of the political aisle. Then, too often among our elected officials, we have in place of dialogue and discussion among statesmen the incessant bickering and boastfulness of bullies and brutes.

Do you ever feel like the world is getting worse? As one older adult confided in me, "Rabbi, thank God I'm old. I can't keep watching the world spin out of control like this!" Because of the 24/7 news cycle and the torturous incursion of social media into our lives, it becomes easy to lose track of how good we actually have it. So, if you are blessed because you have everything in life that you need, will you say the word "amen"? It's okay; say it out loud: *amen*! Similarly, if you feel grateful for your family or your friends, can I get a *halleluyah!* On the one hand we have everything we could need and most of what we want. Yet, on the other hand, we feel like the world is getting worse every day. We are living in a world out of balance.

It is plainly evident to me that, regarding the world around us, so many of us are growing either angrier or more frightened as each day passes. We seek more and more to live in isolating "safe spaces," physically and spiritually distraught by what those who differ from us have to say. We spend more and more time speaking only in our echo chambers, surrounding ourselves with people who share the same opinions. We become protective about our chosen political parties and defend them as if they are our religion, or the contrary: we struggle to find a place among the current political system because it feels as if no one is giving voice to our perspectives. Friendships have been affected and families split because of the sharpness of our rhetoric and the strength of our opinions. We believe that those who disagree with us must be totally ignorant, entirely idiots, or worse: simply evil.

Indeed, the world does feel out of balance. Two thousand years ago, in the midst of the Roman occupation of Jerusalem, the fall of the Holy Temple, and later the forced exile from our land, the rabbis knew about a world out of balance. In the midst of that chaos and suffering, the great sage Rabbi Shimon ben Gamliel taught, "The world stands on three things: on truth, on justice, and on peace."[4] For the sake of balance, like one sitting upon a

4. Pirkei Avot 1:18.

stool, the world needs three legs, and if one of those legs were to falter, society as we know it would come crashing down. And so, the rabbi taught, "The world stands on three things: on truth, on justice, and on peace."

Because of our faith in God, we believe that the nature of truth is binary—a statement of fact is either accurate or it is inaccurate; it is right, or it is wrong. Certainly, we might not be able to ascertain the truth, but we accept that truth exists and that ultimately God is in possession of it.

Justice, though, is nonbinary: it exists on a sliding scale. As we assess the totality of facts that we possess, we do our best to make a decision: to take a stand somewhere on a particular issue. In forming conclusions about significant matters, each of us must seek to perform God's will on earth while at the same time realizing that, unlike God, we are imperfect; we are subject to error. The awareness of our imperfection, therefore, ought to lead us to humility in offering our perspectives. As believers, we cannot abdicate our efforts to achieve justice, but we recognize that, unlike truth, our efforts are subject to human fallibility. "Who is wise?" Ben Zoma taught us two thousand years ago. "One who learns from all people."[5]

Yet, *how many* people are seeking to learn from others' knowledge and insight? In today's world, the notion of truth as binary and justice as nonbinary is inverted: facts and data are interpreted, and sometimes even rejected outright in favor of the conclusion we *want* to be right. More than a decade ago, the satirical news anchor Stephen Colbert labeled this phenomenon "truthiness," which the *Merriam-Webster* online dictionary now defines as "truth that comes from the gut, not books" and "the quality of preferring concepts or facts one wishes to be true, rather than concepts or facts known to be true."[6]

But as Colbert reminds us, whether it is the New York Times or Fox News, whether it is the words of a Republican leader or a Democratic leader, more often than not we are hearing and then

5. Pirkei Avot 4:1.
6. "Truthiness."

rendering assessments of the world based on truthiness rather than on truth. Then we gather with anyone who will listen and agree, and we dismiss outright all those who have opposing thoughts. It is no surprise then that because the notions of truth as binary and justice as nonbinary are inverted that the legs of the three-legged stool are out of place. The world is indeed out of balance.

Rabbi Shimon ben Gamliel taught, "The world stands on three things: truth, justice, and peace." But in society today, it is not just two legs of the three-legged stool that are off kilter; the leg of peace, too, has gone awry. This, though, has been true throughout history. When God created humankind, God designed our nature to be ill at ease. More specifically, our brains, as an ancient safety mechanism, are designed to overreact to potential threats or to overrespond to threats that have passed.

When, for example, we are on an El Al flight from Toronto to Tel Aviv for our children's first trip to Israel (which we were), and the engine explodes (which it did), even though we land safely we become for a time fearful of flying (or at least I did). When we have a bad meal at a restaurant, especially if it makes us sick, we stop eating at that restaurant entirely. When, as my youngest son did, you try to catch a bee in your hand and then you get stung, you stop trying to catch bees. Though for my young son, he did have to learn this lesson the hard way—twice. Then we also have ancient fear triggers built into our collective memory. When we see a spider or a snake and then jump three feet into the air, it is a response to an ancient signal in our brain that warns us of danger. To put it another way, God instilled within human nature systems by which we keep ourselves safe at the expense of a sense of peace, and therefore the leg of peace attached to the stool upon which the world stands has always been somewhat wobbly. But now, in the modern world, that leg is even less secure and so we are feeling less and less at peace.

Case in point: while the media is essential to a strong democracy, the media sells newspapers and advertisements by playing into our fear system and into our primitive love for a juicy story. Though I do not believe the news industry to be malicious, in the 24/7 news cycle we are learning of fewer cats rescued from trees or the good works of children trying to make a difference, and instead we are hearing constantly about human tragedies, political conflict, and impending potential weather catastrophes. Sometimes it feels as if the media is just trying to show us a good fight rather than provide us with accurate, multisided information. Truthiness sells better than truth.

And, while the media might be financially motivated to capitalize on our fears rather than doing so out of malice, there are individuals—racists, anti-Zionists, and the "occasional" politician on both sides of the aisle, for example—who stoke human fears by perpetuating misinformation and half-truths and repeating lies often enough that, in humanity's ingrained tendency toward fear, we actually start to believe and to follow the anger and the evil. Because in our day we negate truth and draw conclusions of justice based on incomplete data, our fear systems lead us to render quick opinions to the extreme left and to the extreme right about topics as broad as refugees and immigrants, about international relations and terrorism, about gender identification and minorities, about the environment and the economy, about Middle East peace, and about the potential for war with North Korea or Iran, China or Russia.

Our innate tendency to overdramatize our sense of fear means that even if truth and justice were in balance, we are constantly striving to compensate for our lack of feelings of peace. But now, when truth and justice are out of whack as well, it feels as if the entire world is out of balance—as if society is collapsing around us. But is that true? Is society really collapsing around us?

Reasons to Hope

Perhaps then you will be reassured to know that in the last twenty years, the proportion of the population living in extreme poverty has been cut in half. Now don't get me wrong, there are still more than a billion people on Earth living in extreme poverty. They need our help, for sure; but humankind's efforts toward advancement, development, and addressing the plight of those who are in need are actually and truly making a difference.

Another data point to consider: tragically, in 2016, 4.2 million children died before the age of one. It's a staggering number. That many children dying before the age of one is way too many; it's just terrible, especially when many of those deaths were preventable. This statistic alone might lead us to conclude that, indeed, the world is getting worse. But, in the previous year, 4.4 million children died and in the year before that, 4.5 million. In 1950, though, 14.4 million children died before the age of one. That's an improvement today by ten million children.[7]

More good news: drastically fewer people die today in war or from natural disasters. Research reveals that "people around the world believe in gender equality more than ever before, and more value religious freedom. Poverty, malnutrition, illiteracy, child labor and infant mortality are all on the decline."[8] The data shows that the world is actually getting healthier, wealthier, and safer. The threats of war, famine, and plague are—statistically speaking on their way toward eradication.[9] This is great news!

Now, please don't get me wrong: there are real problems that need to be addressed. We have not eradicated war; we have not eliminated poverty or ended famine; God knows we have not cured every disease or affliction. We certainly have not ended discrimination or prejudice—against women, against Jews, against the LGBTQ+ community, against African Americans or others. There is plenty of work yet to be done. But overall, we must find some sense of satisfaction in knowing that our efforts toward caring for those who are in need are succeeding and, rather than resting on our laurels, that satisfaction should embolden us to work harder. We confronted the worst pandemic in a century and, in less than two years, created vaccines and medicine to address it! But it is human nature to quickly forget the success stories and to focus instead just on the tragedies. Then again, because of our

7. Rosling et al., *Factfulness*, 15.

8. Rosling et al., *Factfulness*, 130–31.

9. See, for example, Harari, *Homo Deus*.

short-term memory of successes, perhaps we are blessedly more inclined to get involved when a natural disaster strikes; just ask the Israelis, who are always among the first nations to send support to another country with tragedy falls.

Through giant leaps in technology and through individual acts of loving-kindness, the world is getting better even if we struggle to believe it. When God formed that covenant with Abraham some four thousand years ago, God and Abraham together changed the course of human history: no longer is time a perpetual circle of birth, marriage, children, and death, or a never-ending cycle of planting, growing, and harvesting. Rather, because of the covenant, time can be perceived as a spiral with a beginning point and an end point. Yes, we continue to celebrate the cycle of life and experience the agricultural year, but since God and Abraham struck that covenant, the world is on a path toward betterment and we are on a journey that ought to be filled with hope.[10] Put more religiously, every year we are getting closer to the messianic era so long as we walk in God's ways, perform the commandments, and demonstrate compassion toward our fellow human beings. And every day we can get closer to a sense of balance, so long as we are committed to the teaching of Rabbi Shimon ben Gamliel: "The world stands on three things: on truth, on justice, and on peace."

Because of the inversion of truth and justice and because of our biological tendency toward fear, our world is indeed out of balance, but it must not be without hope. When we uphold truth as binary—when we correct errors of fact and hold others accountable to do the same—we bring balance back to the world. When we humbly recognize that the judgments we make are less than perfect and actively seek other perspectives that may even contradict our own, we bring balance back to the world.

And truth and judgment are only two of the three legs. We must also pursue peace. Where there is suffering, we must be a source of compassion. Where there is complacency, we must be a source of activism. Where there is misinformation, we must be a source of factualism. Where there is anger, we must be a source of

10. Cahill, *Gift of the Jews*.

75

reason. Where there is godlessness, we must be a source of godliness. And where there is fear, we must be a source of hope. In so doing, we bring balance back to the world. This is why we learn that a true hero is one who overcomes his or her animal nature to instead ascend toward reason and toward humility, toward kindness and toward compassion, toward faith and toward hope.[11] In Judaism, a hero isn't one who lacks fear; a hero is someone who, with faith and with perseverance, overcomes his or her fears for the betterment of himself or herself and for the betterment of humankind. We must pursue truth, justice, and peace, and to support our efforts, we must keep faith in God, in ourselves, and in the goodness of humankind.

In Psalm 27:13–14, the psalm Jews recite during season of repentance, we read, "I remain confident of this: I will see the goodness of the ETERNAL in the land of the living. Place your hope in the ETERNAL; be strong and take courage and place your hope in the ETERNAL." We do indeed live in a world that is out of balance. But through courage and through hope, through action and through faith, we are obligated to bring balance back.

To be the adult children of God is to rededicate ourselves to gratitude for the blessings we have and to the obligation of fulfilling the ritual commandments that give us meaning by deepening our sense of the Divine's presence in our lives. To be the adult children of God also means that we strive to fulfill the ethical commandments that give us purpose by bringing comfort to the afflicted among us. In the midst of that too, to be the adult children of God means that we double our own efforts toward joyful living.

The Jewish Obligations to Remember and to Remind

When we accept that we are God's adult children, we accept that it is our job to act as God would act in this world. We are obligated to care for those who are in need and we are obligated to pursue truth, justice, and peace. In addition, we are obligated to be in

---

11. Pirkei Avot 4:1.

relationship with our Heavenly Parent. We are also obligated to remember and to remind.

With that in mind, we must admit: we do not listen enough to old people anymore; it is one of the great sins of twenty-first-century America, but those who actively belong to faith communities generally listen to the elderly better than most others. We honor the aged, and I am grateful. My synagogue family, Congregation Shaarey Zedek of Southfield, Michigan, embraced my grandfather through-and-through. I am grateful to them for the kindness that they showed him in life: for celebrating his birthdays with us at the synagogue; for allowing me to reflect on his life during sermons; for the handshakes, the hugs, and the friendship that they offered him each Shabbat morning; and for listening to his story—his important story—as a Holocaust survivor, of course, and also as an old man.

Mindful of the powerful gift and obligation of memory, Rabbi Morris Adler wrote, "We thank Thee, O God of life and love for the resurrecting gift of memory which endows Thy children fashioned in Thy image with the God-like sovereign power to give immortality through love." The rabbi concluded his prayer, "Blessed be Thou, O God, who enablest Thy children to remember."[12]

For my grandfather, Wolf Gruca (may he rest in peace), memory was his blessing and his curse. Throughout his 101 years, Grandpa remembered everything. He could not only recite to you the names of every family member murdered by the Nazis eighty years ago, but he could recite Polish poetry that he learned in grade school and, even after he crossed the century mark, he could tell me the address of the cousin living in New York to whom Grandpa wrote in 1945 and who helped bring my grandfather to America. He remembered the love of his parents and could until the very end tell story after story of their kindness. Then, not just those ancient memories, but even at 101 years old he remembered without hesitation the names of all his great-grandchildren, and he could even identify my voice over the telephone with a mere, "Hi, Grandpa." A sound memory was one of the gifts my grandfather celebrated.

12. Quoted in Rank and Freeman, *Moreh Derech*, E-94.

It was that same gift of memory, however, that also forced him to relive night after night the horrors of the Holocaust: memories so difficult that he refused to share many of them out loud with us. Grandpa remembered attending before the war two different synagogues, and he remembered that on the evening leading into Yom Kippur, Kol Nidre, in the year that the Nazis were advancing on Poland, that not only were the women crying, and not only were the men crying, but "even the walls were crying" (which I hear in his thick Polish accent in which "walls" sounds more like "valls").

Rabbi Adler was right in that the ability to remember does indeed grant to us humans the power to give immortality: when we live on through the memories of others it is like we continue to be alive. Sometimes, though, and with all due respect to Rabbi Adler, when life has given us sadness and suffering, abuse and persecution, the ability to remember is also a shackle from which we pray for freedom. If I might humbly add to Rabbi Adler's prayer, I might suggest that in addition to thanking God, that we also plead with God for the ability to celebrate the joyful memories and the wisdom to grow from the difficult memories, the inspiration to give thanks for the memories that uplift and the strength to find meaning in even the memories that cause us pain.

The Fragility of Memory and the Commandment to Remember

Though the Bible frequently tells us that God, like my grandfather, remembers everything and everyone, most of us humans are plagued with short and often inaccurate memories. As an antidote to the global human tendency to unwittingly forget the kindness shown to us by others or to intentionally alter memories because of our hubris, we are commanded to remember and we are also commanded to remind, sometimes as a basis for faith and sometimes to express compassion for our friends and family. We read in chapter after chapter that God freed us from slavery to remember that God is present in our lives and that God's presence ensures that we as individuals and we as a people are never alone. We are reminded too of God's compassion, especially for those who are sick and those who are mourning, as well as God's joy for those who are celebrating marriages and the arrival of new generations. Our memories of God's righteousness, compassion, and faithfulness should inspire our own acts of righteousness, compassion, and faithfulness.

I do not think it a coincidence that the first of the Ten Commandments and the fifth commandment resemble each other. "I am the ETERNAL your God who brought you out of the land of Egypt, the house of bondage," we read in Exodus 20:2 and Deuteronomy 5:6. Of course, God simply could have self-identified by the holy four-letter name, reminding us that God is the singular deity. Then the text adds, however, a description of the miracle par excellence of the Hebrew Bible. God does not want us to forget what was done for the Israelites, especially when we had arrived in the land of Israel and everything was going well. God does not want to be forgotten when the Israelites no longer perceive a day-to-day need for God's help.

Similarly, we read in Exodus 20:12 and Deuteronomy 5:16, "Honor your father and your mother." This is not a commandment specifically given to minor children to say "please" and "thank you" when their folks feed them. Rather, this is a commandment to grown adults who might otherwise disregard the myriad ways in which their parents cared for them because they—the adult children—can now provide for themselves. This commandment, one of the Top Ten, specifically requires adult children to show the proper deference and appreciation for their parents and, even more, to provide for the parents just as the parents once provided for the children. Just as God does not want to be forgotten, God reminds us not to forget about our parents either. In both the first and the fifth commandments, we are instructed that even though time has passed, and we are no longer in need of the same level of support, "don't forget to call home."

Remember Your Fragility So as to Care for Others

In addition to remembering that we are in possession of a unique and special relationship with God, the five books of Moses reminds us thirty-six times to remember that we were strangers in a strange land. In reminding us of our historical fragility, the Bible demands that if we become powerful, then we are forbidden from oppressing or even taking advantage of others who are weaker; likewise, when we have all that we need, we are obligated to provide to others who are without. In our faith and with our joy, we remember how it feels to suffer, and so we are commanded to give generously, to practice justice, and to show abundant kindness.

"You shall not mistreat or oppress a foreigner, for you were foreigners in the land of Egypt," Exodus 22:20 instructed our ancestors. Adding again one chapter later, Exodus 23:9 reads, "You shall not oppress a foreigner, for you know the soul of the foreigner because you were foreigners in the land of Egypt." In Leviticus 19:33, we are instructed, "When a foreigner dwells among you in your land, you shall not mistreat him." Four chapters later, Leviticus 23:22 reads, "When you reap the harvest of your land, do not reap all the way to the edges of your field or gather the gleanings of your harvest; for the poor and for the stranger you shall leave them." The Bible demonstrates clearly that memory not only forms the nation's identity, but it also creates a justification and motivation to care for others in similar circumstances.

Just as significant as reminding the people Israel of their obligation to care for the strangers among them, Deuteronomy also obligates the nation's leaders to adhere to these moral principles. "When [the Israelite king] is seated on his sovereign throne, he shall have written for himself a copy of this Teaching, inscribed for him on a scroll by the Levitical priests. It should remain with him so that he can read in it all his life, and learn to revere the ETERNAL his God, to observe faithfully every word of this Teaching as well as these laws." Moses then explains the reason for this unusual law: "Thus [the king] will not elevate himself above his fellows or turn from the law to the right or to the left, so that he and his descendants may reign a long time in the midst of Israel" (Deut 17:18-20). The Israelites' memory of their oppression in Egypt obligates them to treat the strangers living among them in a way diametrically opposed to how the Egyptians treated them.

The prophet Jeremiah lived some 2,500 years ago, in the midst of the destruction of the First Holy Temple. Through blood and tears our ancestors wondered how God could seemingly abandon them. They cried out to God desperate to understand their suffering. And, through Jeremiah, God responds. "If you really mend your ways and your actions," we read, "if you execute justice between one person and another; if you do not oppress the stranger, the orphan, and the widow; if you do not shed the blood of the innocent in this place; if you do not follow other gods, to your own hurt—then," God tells Jeremiah, "then will I let you dwell in this place, in the land that I (God) gave to your ancestors for all time" (Jer 7:5-7). Because of our experience in Egypt, we know what it is like to be the powerless. Thus, the Bible teaches us that the pursuit of justice is ensuring that the powerful do not take advantage of those with lesser power. God reminds us that when we possess power, we must pursue justice by bringing equality to unequal situations.

In an addendum to the biblical take on justice, the Talmud tells of an interesting story based on a different verse in the Bible. In the book of Isaiah, God refers twice to God's own house of prayer. The rabbis look to this text and ask these questions: (1) God prays? (2) For what could God possibly pray? Of course, humans pray to God. But for what could God pray? Rabbi Zutra then comes forward and suggests the prayers that come from God's metaphorical heart. God prays to God's self: "May it be my will that my compassion overcomes my anger, and that my compassion prevails over my [other] attributes too, so that I may deal with my children compassionately and, on their behalf, stop short of the limit of strict justice."[13] In other words, God prays that compassion supersedes fairness. God prays that acts of mercy overtake even the great pursuit of justice. The messages of our Bible and the

13. b. Ber. 7a.

rabbis are clear that we must fill our hearts with compassion and, especially when we possess any form of power, we must remember what it means to go without and thus we are obligated to act with kindness, fairness, and truth.

Remember Your Fragility So as to Not Become Fragile Again

At the same time, we are also commanded to remember our fragility so that we do not allow our fragility to lead to our demise. "Remember" and "never forget" Deuteronomy tells us (Deut 25:17–19). Abraham, the first wandering Jew, was a nomad who traveled the fertile crescent of the ancient world from modern-day Iraq north and west to Turkey, in search of stability and a secure future. It was then that God appeared to Abraham and, in exchange for accepting a covenant of faith, Abraham received land and children: stability and a future. Abraham's leap of faith earned him a physical and emotional sense of home.

Similarly, when the Israelites were in Egypt, they experienced the plight of national homelessness. Freed from physical torture and spiritual oppression, the Israelites' exodus became the ultimate miracle of history: the return of a displaced people to their home, to their freedom, to their safety, to their opportunity to forge a nation based on the values they hold dear.

The thesis of this book is that, like the Parent of adult children, God has withdrawn from this world in order to allow humans to act: to live in the way in which God wants us to live. The greatest challenge to this thesis, I believe, is actually the birth of the State of Israel in 1948.

In a demonstration that perhaps miracles continue to happen in our own day, the Jewish people began coming home a little more than a century ago, as the early Zionist pioneers began the process of restoring the land of Israel for the people Israel. In the late 1890s, the French government wrongly accused a Jewish Frenchman and military officer named Alfred Dreyfus of treason. A young Theodore Herzl was a journalist at his trial, and after witnessing this open act of anti-Semitism, Herzl concluded that the Jews needed a place of their own in order to permanently escape centuries of Jew-hatred. Herzl realized that if the enlightened and emancipated France failed to protect an assimilated and loyal Jewish officer, the rest of Europe would be no different; the Jews needed to leave. Herzl intensified his Zionist efforts, organized like-minded leaders, and became the father of political Zionism.

In the midst of those discussions on how best to solve the Jewish problem, another writer—Asher Hirsch Tzvi Ginsburg or, as he was known by his pen name, Achad HaAm—saw the world differently. Achad HaAm challenged Herzl's notion that anti-Semitism represented the biggest threat to Jews. Achad HaAm saw the biggest threat to the Jews as assimilation—that is, in a westernized Europe the Jews would feel so comfortable that they would give up their Judaism entirely. Theodor Herzl worried that the Jews would never find a home anywhere but Israel. Achad HaAm worried that the Jews would feel so much at home outside their own land that they would stop being Jewish, which, for Achad HaAm, was not necessarily about God, but also about culture: about food, about language, about relationship, about how to live an ethical life. Of course, though Herzl and Achad HaAm held very different fears, their solutions intersected around the idea that the Jews needed a land of their own: a physical haven from anti-Semitism and also a spiritual wellspring from which to draw their creative energy. Though Theodor Herzl and Achad HaAm had very different motivations for rebuilding Israel as a Jewish nation, they both agreed that the Jews needed their own home.

Fast forward and we are now more than a century after the Dreyfus affair and three-quarters of a century into Israel's existence as a Jewish state. The Holocaust proved Herzl correct: the Jews could never be at home—could never be physically safe—anywhere but their own land. Interestingly, the twenty-first century is now also proving Achad HaAm correct: when given freedom and the opportunity to assimilate, Jews will. We will cast off our Judaism as quickly as the non-Jewish world will allow us. In many ways, then, Israel has come to fulfill Achad HaAm's mission as well. Not only is Israel a physical haven—a homeland—for Jews, but today Israel is also the home in which we come to understand our place in the eternal story of the Jewish people and Judaism: a story that goes back to Abraham, that continues through the Exodus, and that bring us to today and beyond. Any Jew who has been to Israel knows that feeling of at-homeness. We get what it means to be part of something bigger than ourselves. And, I believe, it is only when we find our place in a collective narrative that one can feel true meaning in life.

In so many ways, then, for Jews, Israel's existence and its role as a center of Jewish thought can offer us an opportunity to find our place in the eternal story of the Jewish people. "For out of Zion shall go forth the Torah and the word of God from Jerusalem" (Isa 2:3).

Yes, we are vulnerable—but we are not victims. We remember our fragility so that others do not suffer, and we remember our fragility in order to protect ourselves as well.

To Remember and to Remind

"Remember and never forget," Deut 25:17–19 reminds us. "Remember and never forget" is our job living after the Holocaust too. We Jews remember that no one stood up for us when we most needed it and so we have to stand up for ourselves. We remember too how it feels to suffer, and thus we remember to care deeply for others, to practice justice, and to act mercifully. Non-Jews remember what happened when they stood silent, when they waited for someone else to act to alleviate the suffering. In turn, the good and decent gentiles of this world reach out across faith traditions to help all who are in need. And now, through our words and through our actions today, we remind the world that it too should do the same.

During his life, Holocaust survivor Wolf Gruca served as a living reminder. Because of those years of slavery and suffering, he reminded us to look forward and not just backward. He reminded us that time is a blessing, and that time with family, friends, and community is the greatest gift of all. And now, in his death, to remember and never forget is what my grandfather Wolf Gruca wanted too, especially from his children, grandchildren, and great-grandchildren. During his last several years, whenever my grandfather would send my kids or me a birthday card, he included with it a letter asking simply that he be remembered. Isn't that, at the end of the day, what we all want: to gain immortality through the memories of our family and our community? When we remember those who came before, when we remember especially all the survivors of the Holocaust, we grant them true immortality.

For me, personally, I remember my grandfather when I drive by his old neighborhood. We remember him at holiday meals and in quiet moments of reflection. We remember him when we celebrate weddings, bar mitzvahs, and baby naming ceremonies, and we remember him when times are challenging too. Even in my grandfather's silence, we remember him; we cherish him; we recall him wisdom; and we give thanks to him for all the blessings he provided us.

So, in memory of Wolf Gruca, I pray along with Rabbi Adler: "We thank Thee, O God of life and love for the resurrecting gift of memory which endows Thy children fashioned in Thy image with the God-like sovereign power to give immortality through love." To this, I add, "Please, God, grant us also the ability to celebrate the joyful memories and the wisdom to grow from the difficult memories, the inspiration to give thanks for the memories that uplift and the strength to find meaning in even the memories that cause us pain." And we finished with Rabbi Adler's words again: "Blessed be Thou, O God, who enablest Thy children to remember and who commands us to remind."[14]

---

14. Quoted in Rank and Freeman, *Moreh Derech*, 94.

8

Joy

GOD WANTS US TO live a life of gratitude. God wants us to live a life of obligation. God also wants us to live a life of joy. The story is told of a cat who died and went to heaven.

> God met her at the gates and said, "You have been a good cat all these years. Anything you want is yours for the asking."
>
> The cat thought for a minute and then said, "All my life I lived on a farm and slept on hard wooden floors. I would like a real fluffy pillow to sleep on."
>
> God said, "Say no more." Instantly the cat had a huge fluffy pillow.
>
> A few days later, six mice were killed in an accident and they all went to Heaven together. God met the mice at the gates with the same offer that [God] made to the cat.
>
> The mice said, "Well, we have had to run all of our lives: from cats, dogs, and even people with brooms! If we could just have some little roller skates, we would not have to run again."
>
> God answered, "It is done." All the mice had beautiful little roller skates.

About a week later, God decided to check on the cat. [God] found her sound asleep on her fluffy pillow. God gently awakened the cat and asked, "Is everything okay? How have you been doing? Are you happy?"

The cat replied to God, "Oh, it is WONDERFUL. I have never been so happy in my life. The pillow is so fluffy, and those little Meals on Wheels that you have been sending over are delicious!"[1]

Turns out, one person's happiness is not necessarily another's. Interestingly, the word "happy" seems to derive from the word "luck"; "happ" meaning "chance or fortune" as in *what happens* to us. We still see the meaning in the modern words "happenstance," "hapless," and "perhaps." The cat from the story was happy because of the good luck sent her way.

Happiness. It's a complicated emotion. Are you happy? For real—right here, right now—are you happy? Or, perhaps more importantly, when was the last time you asked your spouse, your child, your friend: are you happy? And is your sense of happiness, like the cat, the result of luck—of that which *has happened* to you? Health instead of illness, success instead of failure, wealth instead of poverty, joy instead of sorrow—are we happy only when times seem good, or do times seem good simply because we are happy?

When God tells Abraham to take his beloved son Isaac and to offer him as a sacrifice to the ETERNAL, Abraham—the man who argued with God to prevent the suffering of innocents at Sodom and Gomorrah—remains throughout the story of the binding, seemingly devoid of emotion. Rather, we hear mostly only about Abraham's actions. "Abraham woke up early," Genesis reads, "he saddled his donkey . . . he split wood for the burnt offering . . . he set out for the land that God told him" (Gen 22:3).

Was Abraham happy at receiving God's call? Joyful in being able to serve the ETERNAL? Or was Abraham angry that God would tell him to sacrifice his little boy? Was Abraham sad? Scared? Curious? Proud? Upon hearing of his wife Sarah's death, we learn that Abraham cried for her a torrent of tears; his heart

---

1. "Meaning of True Happiness."

was broken (Gen 23:2). But when told to slaughter his son? We hear nothing; not a word. Not once are we told of our patriarch's emotions, simply that he was following God's instructions. "Abraham took the wood for the burnt offering . . . he took the firestone and the knife . . . and he walked together with his son" (Gen 22:6).

A plain reading of Genesis seems to suggest that Isaac might have been a child when he walked up that lonely mountain with his father. In my head I picture a small boy, perhaps dark curly hair, a broad smile on his face in having the chance to enjoy an extended camping trip with his daddy. "The two of them walked together" (Gen 22:6). Isn't childhood, after all, about the simple joys of life? About swimming in the neighborhood pool on a hot summer day? About tossing the football with friends late into the evening come fall? About snuggling up with a warm cup of hot chocolate after hours of wintertime sledding? If children are provided with their basic needs, including love and a life free from abuse, aren't most children generally—like I picture young Isaac—happy? Aren't they lighthearted and of good cheer?

Yet, the midrash reads our Torah differently. For our rabbis, Isaac was a young man of thirty-seven,[2] entirely aware of what he was doing, where he was going with his father, and why. Was he, the thirty-seven-year-old Isaac, giddy like a schoolboy? Euphoric at the fulfillment of his destiny? What about you at thirty-seven years of age: were you bursting with joy, contentment, satisfaction? According to a recent survey, nearly three-quarters of us believe that the happiest year of our lives was . . . age thirty-three. At thirty-three apparently, "innocence has been lost, but our sense of reality is mixed with a strong sense of hope. We have yet to develop the cynicism and world-weariness that comes with later years."[3] While the good news might be we had such a happy year, the bad news is, for most of us here, age thirty-three is more than just a few years ago. We have long since passed our happiest year. At age thirty-seven, ascending the mountain with his father and with full

2. Bereishit Rabbah 57:8.

3. Morales and Siemaszko, "Survey Finds," para. 7.

knowledge of the knife that waited for him, Isaac had long since passed his happiest year as well.

Whether, then, at thirty-three, or thirty-seven, or at some other point in time, how many of us have thought:

> From the outside, you'd think I have it all: beautiful house, wonderful children, devoted [spouse]. But am I happy? I think so. There's nothing that has gone terribly wrong. There's no reason for me not to be happy. But I don't feel happy so much as I feel I'm just going through the motions. Sometimes I have a feeling that there's more and I just haven't found it yet. But what . . . and how dare I want more? Isn't all that I have enough?[4]

What then is that "more" we seek? Do we sometimes yearn for the carefree bliss of childhood exemplified by summer camp, or the indestructibility and self-confidence of that weekend partying experience in college? Are we sometimes envious of the twenty-seven-year-old mother's elation in becoming a new parent or in the seventy-five-year-old looking at his grandchild's smile, confident in the immortality that a next generation represents? But we know too well that summer camp and college tailgating come to an end. The new joy of parenthood gives way to sleepless nights and countless bills. A grandparent's pleasure can, sadly, be diminished by his own failing health and frailty. Yet, despite this, we often define happiness as that particular feeling at a particular moment in time. In other words, if I asked you again the question, "are you happy?" the answer would depend entirely on your state of mind right now—whether, perhaps, a spouse or child is sitting next to you or whether that seat once contained a loved one who has gone to his or her eternal home. It depends on whether you feel ready for your lunch guests who are coming over in just a matter of minutes, or the quality of the dinner to which you are heading shortly.

Happiness might depend on traffic today or the extent of the burden of dressing in the morning. It depends on the last phone call we received, the holiday coming up, or the University of

4. Danziger and Birndorf, *Nine Rooms*, 9.

Michigan's chances at making it to the championship game this year. But it is amazing how easily a football game or one day's failure at work can change our perception of our happiness.

If pleasure fades, where then do we find lasting joy? "[The wisdom of Scripture] is a tree of life to those who hold fast to it, and whoever holds on to [that wisdom] is happy," declares Proverbs 3:18. Or perhaps you prefer Psalm 34: "Happy is the person who trusts in [the ETERNAL]." Psalm 32: "Happy is one whose transgression is forgiven." Proverbs 3: "Happy is the person who finds wisdom." Psalm 41: "Happy is one who is thoughtful of the poor." Psalm 106: "Happy are those who act justly, who do right at all times." Proverbs 20: "The just person walks with integrity, happy are his children after him."

In fact, the Bible speaks so frequently of happiness one must ask: is this why God put us here on Earth—to be happy? A young couple newly in love might answer one way; a poor man living on the street might answer differently. I wonder how you might answer, today, given all that has happened to you in your life: Did God put us on earth . . . to be happy?

In the last few years, a growing number of scholarly articles has come to examine the relationship between religion and mental health, and the research comes to vouch for the Bible's advice. These studies show that people who practice their religion are less depressed, less anxious, and less worried than nonreligious people. They are better able to cope with such crises as illness, divorce, and bereavement. It seems that the more people incorporate religion into daily life—regularly attending worship services, reading the Bible, praying or meditating—the more positive emotions they experience and the more satisfied they are with their lives.[5]

Research has come also to show that social isolation is as big a risk factor for premature death as is smoking[6] and, perhaps, it was early awareness of the human need for relationships that led to gathering in community becoming a central expression of faith. And Facebook and FaceTime are not the same as face-to-face.

5. Lemonick, "Biology of Joy," 46–47.
6. National Academies, *Social Isolation and Loneliness*, 17.

Genesis says that it is not good to be alone, and research shows that married people actually live longer than unmarried people—seven additional years for married men and, well, only four additional years for married women. Exercise, sex, and laughter all reduce stress hormones and enhance the feeling of well-being—and all those actions can be accomplished in the course of a traditional Sabbath experience. Deliberately cultivating a sense of gratitude by counting one's blessings and expressing appreciation to others leads to greater happiness, and faith requires this of us on a daily basis: before and after we eat; when we lie down and when we rise; when we see a rainbow, a special person, a scholar, or an ocean; and even when we go to the bathroom. Research proves that living a religious life can actually make you happier. Remembering to call home is both emotionally and physically good for you too.

Joy, then, and not happiness, comes from building a relationship with God to whom we might turn in difficult times for hope or good times in gratitude. Joy comes from sacrificing time and money for the sake of our community and peoplehood, and especially for those in need. Joy comes from knowing that we have done everything in our power to improve the lives of others. Joy comes from sitting next to our children on the holidays or being aware that they attend services at their own house of worship. Joy comes from participating in ancient rituals, like our parents, grandparents, and ancestors before us. Joy comes from replicating or even enhancing the cherished family recipe passed down from generation to generation. Joy comes from making time each day to learn a little bit more. Joy comes from praying with all our might that tomorrow will be better, safer, healthier, and holier for our families and for us, for Israel, and for all the world.

Research tells us that joy is inspired by performing deeds of kindness, helping others, engaging in meaningful work, and by challenging ourselves—all ways in which we emulate our Heavenly Parent. We come to see that, as my friend Rabbi Scott Nagel teaches, "Seeking happiness is not the purpose of life. Rather, for Judaism, true and enduring happiness (i.e., what I call 'joy') is the by-product of doing those things that *are* the purpose life."[7] We must not be cats sitting on a pillow simply hoping that mice on roller-skates wheel by us. We must live in pursuit of joy.

The Torah tells us that when our father Abraham breathed his last, he was an old man satisfied with his life. He was not caught up in the struggle of finding pleasure day-to-day, but he knew he had made a difference in this world . . . and he was happy. No, strike that: he was joyful. Are you joyful? Truly, deeply joyful? Is your spouse? Your friend? Your child? And how recently have you asked the question of those whom you love? How recently have you sought to find that lasting joy . . . together? Are you . . . joyful?

7. Nagel, "Positivity of Happiness."

But Don't Forget to Call Home

9

How We Call Home

IN OUR MOST CHALLENGING times, and in our happiest times too, we long to feel the helping hand of the divine. As we age, too, we often want to feel part of something bigger and more enduring. Perhaps, though, we are pursuing this relationship with our Heavenly Parent in the wrong ways. Rather than waiting for God to reach out to us, perhaps God is gifting us our freedom and waiting for us to reach out to her/him.

In an interesting inversion of roles, a certain spiritual leader[1] invited his followers to reach out to God the way a parent might look for a child who is hiding. His invitation is rooted in a particular verse from Jeremiah (13:17) in which the prophet gives us God's lament: "'My soul,' says God, 'weeps in secret places.'" The spiritual leader explained this verse by referring to an encounter he had with his grandchild. "[My grandson] asked me to play hide-and-seek with him and I agreed. I closed my eyes and counted, and he went to hide. I was suddenly distracted by a friend and forgot all about the child. Soon I heard him crying from his hiding place, 'No one has come to look for me.'" The spiritual leader, contemplating

1. The Rebbe of Miedzyboz, Poland, 1753–1811, was a grandson of the Baal Shem Tov.

95

his grandson's dismay at no one searching for him, concluded, "So does God cry in [God's] secret place: 'No one comes to look for Me.' The [Master of the World] is waiting for us to seek [God] out." Then the spiritual leader added, "[God] is now more accessible than [God] has been in the last two thousand years. Let us search for [God]—together."[2]

My challenge to us is similar, though I employ a different metaphor. God is the empty-nester Parent of adult children waiting for the children to call, and our method for communication with God is through the expression of our faith. Indeed, faith is a gift and a tool that is, I believe, just as important today as it was thousands of years ago when Judaism—and thus monotheism—first entered the world. That said, though, a twenty-first-century faith requires maturity of mind and spirit. A twenty-first-century faith requires a reconception of our relationship with God; humanity has changed since that day when God first called to Abraham, and thus our understanding of our relationship with God must change too. Like an adult child who desires to honor aging parents, a twenty-first-century faith necessitates embracing the power and responsibility of human autonomy while, simultaneously, welcoming the comfort and support that a relationship with God provides. Moreover, a twenty-first-century faith requires the realization that we best honor our Creator when, as the old proverb goes, we "pray as if everything depended upon God, but act as if everything depended on you."

As young children, we often believe our parents to be omnipotent and omniscient. When we enter our teenage years, however, sometimes we wonder how our parents can even function given how "little" they know and understand! Then, when we enter adulthood, we often begin to realize how strong and wise our parents are; recognizing our fallibility as humans, we forgive our parents their mistakes and shortcomings as we strive to live up to and celebrate their best qualities.

Likewise, as children, we seek a God who is omnipotent, omniscient, and benevolent. However, when the challenges of

2. Lamm, "Face of God," 136.

life happen as they inevitability do, we begin to lose faith because the experience of life does not match our understanding of an all-powerful and all-good God. So, as we age, faith is often lost. But like learning to see our parents through adult eyes, as we age, a more mature faith can be found. God is not the judge on high writing and sealing in a book of life and death, whose hands are involved in every detail on earth. Rather, perhaps God is the parent who, while remaining ever present for wisdom or to lend a helping hand, has sent us as adults out into the world to succeed and to make a difference. God is quietly cheering us on, hoping that we remember God's expectations of us to pursue justice, to act with kindness, and to take care of our brothers and sisters. That is, after all, part of our mission: pursue justice, act with kindness, take care of our brothers and sisters . . . and then there is one more thing that God—that our parents—ask of us: to call home.

Build a Sanctuary

To "act as if everything depends on" us is hard work. The fulfillment of the gift of human autonomy is exhausting. Actively caring for others, pursuing justice, seeking peace, and showing compassion are acts that can drain even the most vibrant of individuals. The world is a challenging place and the continued presence of evil saddens us and challenges us to our very core. It is in those moments of sadness and despair, of frustration and disappointment, that we most benefit from "calling home."

When the Israelites encountered God at Mt. Sinai, they experienced a profound closeness and intimacy with our Creator. Yet, the human condition would not allow the Israelites to remain at the peak of the proverbial mountain nor even at the base of that holy mountain. The Israelites needed to continue forward with their journey. God seemingly realized the spiritual vacuum created by the growing distance between the Heavenly Parent and Her children. In turn, God sent a message to the Israelites through Moses: "Let them make me a sanctuary so that I may dwell among them" (Exod 25:8).

We build our sanctuaries because God is near to all who call upon God, and it is easier to call upon God when others are engaging in similar actions. We build our sanctuaries to mark sacred time and to immerse ourselves in sacred scripture. And just as God's presence is not in the mighty wind or the fire or the earthquake (1 Kgs 19:11–12), God's presence is not in the sanctuary itself. Rather, when we create sanctuary, God dwells in us. When we create sanctuary, we find a spirit and an energy that grow from within. When we create sanctuary, we surround ourselves with like-minded journeyers who will strengthen us and whom we can in turn strengthen. When we build actual and metaphorical sanctuaries, then God dwells among us.

Yet, like the Israelites forbidden from remaining at Mt. Sinai, we cannot linger in that bliss and security of sanctuary and must continue forward with the holy work of pursuing justice, offering compassion, and walking humbly. An interesting verse amidst the Exodus story reminds us that, while God can nourish our souls, it is the role of the faithful ones to bring God's mission to fruition on earth.

We read in Exodus 14:10–16, "As Pharaoh drew near, the Israelites caught sight of the Egyptians advancing upon them. Greatly frightened, the Israelites cried out to the ETERNAL. They said to Moses, 'Was it for want of graves in Egypt that you brought us to die in the wilderness? What have you done to us, taking us out of Egypt?'" Through the leadership of Moses and Aaron, God brought an end to four centuries of slavery and forced Pharaoh's hand to permit the Israelites their freedom. But while the chains were removed from the Israelites' hands and feet, their heads, hearts, and hopes remained bound. So, with the Egyptians at their backs and the mighty reed sea thrashing before them, Moses proclaimed to the newly freed Hebrews, "Have no fear! Stand by and witness the deliverance which the ETERNAL will work for you today; for the Egyptians whom you see today you will never see again." Then Moses added, "The ETERNAL will battle for you; you hold your peace!" Moses tells his people that God will continue to do the hard work for them.

Despite Moses's proclamation, though, God makes clear to the Israelites that, as free men and women, they need to start taking responsibility for the state of world. God reminds the newly freed men and women that they are no longer totally vulnerable children. As such, God responds to Moses's declaration, "Why do you cry out to me? Tell the Israelites to go forward!" When our spiritual fuel tanks get low, we call to God in prayer and we hear God's response through the study of sacred scripture, but we are the ones who still need to act. Prayer and study are at the heart of our call home to our Heavenly Parent. These acts nourish us and sustain us, lifting us when we feel low and brightening us when all we see is the world's darkness. Then, when full again, we remember that it is our job to act on God's behalf to fix a broken world.

When we as God's faithful children struggle in the holy work of pursuing justice, showing compassion, and walking humbly, we remember, "Let them make me a sanctuary so that I may dwell among them" (Exod 25:8). And, after spending some time in that sanctuary, we are reminded, "Why do you cry out to me? Tell the Israelites to go forward!"

10

How We Visit Home

DURING THE SUMMER OF 2020, I was supposed to be in Israel, but given the global pandemic, I spent the summer in a different "holy" city: Southfield, Michigan. I didn't get to post to Facebook one of my favorite sentences: "Leaving home to go home." And so notions of "home" were very much on my mind that COVID summer as I bounced back and forth between feeling totally locked in my house and feeling entirely homeless. On one hand, home is where we feel safe; home is where we set the rules—well, home is where my wife sets the rules, but you understand what I'm saying. Home is where we get to be in charge of our own castle. And in the midst of a global pandemic where even going grocery shopping felt like heading out to war, coming home felt like returning to safety. Did you too share the same relief when you exited the public space to enter the private space? I could wash my hands—twenty seconds with soap and water—and I could take my mask off and breathe. "I'm home."

At the same time though, while "home" gives me an incredible sense of physical safety, throughout much of the pandemic I felt displaced as well. We were living in a *Twilight Zone* episode—a dystopia—where nothing felt quite normal or right; I might even add that, over the last decade with the exponential growth of social media and the 24/7 news industry, I still sometimes feel like I am living in a dystopia. While there were and are places that I can be physically safe, emotionally I feel disjointed, out of sorts, missing the world that was and longing for a return to some sense of normalcy. In many ways, during the COVID-19 pandemic and for the last several years, I've felt . . . homeless.

We Jews know what it means to be without a home. Abraham, the first wandering Jew, was a nomad who traveled the fertile crescent of the ancient world from modern-day Iraq north and west to Turkey, in search of stability and a secure future. It was then that God appeared to Abraham and, in exchange for accepting a covenant of faith, Abraham received land and children: stability and a future. Abraham's leap of faith earned him a physical and emotional sense of home.

Similarly, when our ancestors were in Egypt, they experienced what happens when you are homeless. Tortured physically, oppressed spiritually, their Exodus became the miracle *par excellance* of history: the return of a displaced people to their home. To their freedom. To their safety. To their opportunity to forge a nation based on the values they held dear.

In Deuteronomy, Moses prophesizes for us the recurring story of the Jewish people: exile and return. When we embrace God and turn from our lack of righteousness and our practicing of injustices, then "God will gather you again from all the nations where the ETERNAL your God has scattered you. Even if your exiles are at the ends of the farthest reaches, from there the ETERNAL your God will gather you, from there God will fetch you. And the ETERNAL your God will bring you to the land that your ancestors inherited, and you shall inherit it; and God will make you more prosperous and more numerous than your ancestors," (Deut 30:1–5). That is to say, when we recognize our mistakes toward God and when we improve how we treat each other and care for others including and especially, by the way, the homeless, then God will bring us home from wherever we are. God will bring us home. And this home to which God will bring us is a place of refuge and physical safety; it is a national sanctuary; it is a synagogue without walls in which to serve God with joy and prayer; and it is also a laboratory in which we might strive to create a society that heeds God's calls for justice and for compassion.

God is waiting for us to call home. Through study and through observance, through participating in the communal life of our houses of worship, through taking the necessary steps to pursue justice and through practicing compassion for others, then we are calling home. When we support a secure and peaceful Jewish State of Israel, then we too begin the path toward redemption—we call home. When that happens, as our Torah states, "God will gather you again from all the nations where the ETERNAL your God has scattered you. Even if your exiles are at the ends of the farthest reaches, from there the ETERNAL your God will gather you, from there God will fetch you. And the ETERNAL your God will bring you to the land that your ancestors inherited, and you shall inherit it; and God will make you more prosperous and more numerous than your ancestors," (Deut 30:3–4).

And let us remember that, even more than calling home, it is good to visit too. Especially given the rise of anti-Semitism around the world, Israel continues to serve as a physical haven for Jews anywhere and everywhere. Israel continues to be a place of spiritual rebirth, a place of religious pluralism, and a place from which we can derive from the study of sacred scripture the profound insights into the human condition and a sense of meaning in this chaotic world. And, when as a nation, Israel realizes its mission to be a place of righteousness, justice, and compassion, and when it strives to live up to the prophets' greatest ideals, so then we can proclaim as an entire people, "For from Zion, Instruction (Torah) shall come forth; the word of the ETERNAL from Jerusalem" (Isa 2:2–3).

It is not easy to call home frequently and it is even harder to visit. However, through prayer, through study, and through performing acts of compassion for God's (other) children, then we begin to call home. And when we board a flight to the promised land or even purchase products that were produced there, then we engage in the act of visiting home. And we all would benefit from a little more time at home or calling home, and all the respiritualization that comes from being home with our Heavenly Parent.

11

The Benefits of Calling Home

As ADULTS, WHEN WE call home to our parents, we are offered (in healthy situations) a sheltering and comforting presence. Perhaps more than anything, that is what our parents can do for us as we age and as they age. They can remind us that we are not alone; they can remind us that we are loved; and they can remind us that no matter what happens, someone has our backs.

Likewise, even as empowered adults, we can reach out to God in order to receive from God. In difficult times—after yet another school shooting, for example, or during an illness or at the loss of a loved one—I find myself turning to the words of Psalm 20: "May the ETERNAL answer you in time of trouble; may the God of Jacob be your strength." It is true that in these moments, I am looking for answers to my prayers and, indeed, I am looking for strength. I do not actually believe that God will part the waters for me, but I do believe that God is with me as I dive into the sea. In reciting the psalm, however, we must ask: why would the psalmist call upon the God of Jacob? After all, in Genesis, God promises to be Abraham's Shield (Gen 15:1). So why, in moments of distress and sorrow should I turn to "the God of Jacob"? Why not "the God of Abraham"? Why not, for that matter, the "God of Moses"?

Many of us know the story of Joseph. After the descent of this dreamer into Egypt and then prison, Joseph rises to become second-in-command over all Egypt. He guides the mighty country through its seven years of plenty, all the while preparing for the coming famine. We learn that the famine swept throughout the Middle East and then, two years in, only Egypt has the resources to feed its residents because of Joseph's prophetic planning.

As such, the patriarch Jacob—still living in the promised land—sends his remaining sons into Egypt to acquire food and to bring the sustenance back to the promised land. Quickly, however, the food runs out. The brothers return to Egypt whereupon Joseph reveals his true identity to them. They reconcile; Joseph forgives the brothers and acknowledges that his suffering was all part of God's master plan. Joseph asks his brothers and father to leave the land of Israel and, with Pharaoh's permission, to move to Egypt.

Understandably, Jacob is reluctant to leave Israel. This is when God appears with comforting words to our patriarch: "Fear not to go down to Egypt, for I will make you there into a great nation. I myself will go down with you to Egypt, and I myself will also bring you back" (Gen 46:3–4). In other words, God goes with us into the dark, narrow places (in Hebrew, the word for Egypt, *Mitzrayim,* means "from the narrow places") and God is the one who also guides us out. King David said it similarly in Psalm 23: "Though I walk through the valley of the shadow of death, I shall fear no evil, for Thou art with me."

In times of great tragedy—whether on the national, the local, or the individual level—God journeys with us. We are not alone; we are *never* alone. The God who traveled with the Israelites down into Egypt is the same God that brought us up and back to the promised land. God might be the Shield of Abraham and God might be Redeemer of Moses, but God is also the Hope of Jacob.

We are adults, and God, like our parents, expects us to solve our own problems. Nevertheless, like God reminds Jacob and like Psalm 20 assures us, the God of Jacob will be near. When we are in need of hope—when we need to be reminded that better days lay ahead—we remember to call upon the God of Jacob for hope, for assurance, for comfort, and for love.

Indeed, throughout centuries of war, famine, and plague, faith and hope are the instruments by which humanity has coped. When, throughout history, people perceived themselves entirely powerless, faith and hope seemed their only options. "I believe with perfect faith in the coming of the messiah," Maimonides wrote in his Thirteen Principles of Jewish Faith, "And even though he tarry, still I believe." Like children who are entirely reliant on parents, faith and hope are the sole tools of those who feel entirely dependent on others. Faith and hope are the only instruments of the powerless; well, perhaps also the kindness of others.

As we grow up, however—whether that development is in age or in spirit—we begin to realize that control, autonomy, and agency appear in various forms and are achieved through different avenues. The medieval Rabbi Shlomo Yitzchaki (Rashi) asks why the Bible refers twice to Moses growing up in consecutive verses when it seems redundant. About Moses we read in Exodus 2:10, "When the child grew up, [Yocheved, Moses's mother] brought him to Pharaoh's daughter, who made him her son. [Pharaoh's daughter] named him Moses, explaining, 'I drew him out of the water.'" Here the Torah speaks of Moses's physical development. He came of a certain age; he was taken from his mother; and he was brought to the palace. Immediately in the next verse (Exod 2:11), the Torah teaches, "Then after some time, when Moses had grown up and went out to his kinsfolk, he saw their suffering. He witnessed an Egyptian beating a Hebrew, one of his kinsmen. Turning this way and that way and, seeing no one nearby, he struck down the Egyptian and hid him in the sand." That is to say, upon seeing his people's suffering, Moses "grew up" because he knew that he had to act . . . and so he did. "Growing up" means seizing what control you have and acting for the betterment of one's own life or the lives of others.

From the moment that God chose Abraham, God has been encouraging humanity to "grow up": to find agency in the midst of seeming powerlessness, to embrace life precisely because life is vulnerable. Certainly, as Moses demonstrated, we too grow up by caring for those who are in need. We also grow up by choosing, in the midst of all the craziness of our world, to live lives of meaning and purpose. We grow up by practicing gratitude and by seeking moments of joy. And we grow up when we realize the hope that God places on humanity and we make that hope our own.

When we do that—when we grow and take responsibility for our own lives, our own society, our own world—then we can achieve the adult lives that God wants of us and then God can be to us the way parents relate to adult children: as a source of support, comfort, and love. God can be the model of hopefulness required to continue the journey forward that Abraham began so many thousands of years ago.

Hope

Before we get to hope, though, we often need to walk first through the valley of shadows.

I met Sam when he and his big sister Sophia started preschool at the synagogue that I served. They were cute kids and very sweet. In their home, they referred to religious school as "God school." I always liked that. Even then, Sam and Sophia were smart. Super smart. Even then, they gave deeply of themselves to others. I journeyed with Sophia and Sam as they finished religious school; I stood next to them when they became bat mitzvah and bar mitzvah; and I journeyed with them again as they became teaching assistants in our religious school—in our God school. Through their learning at the synagogue, in their Jewish high school, and through Jewish youth group, they became quite Jewishly knowledgeable and embraced by our community. They collected friends wherever they went, and along with their parents, they worked tirelessly for people in need. Both Sam and Sophia know that their families, their friends, and their people all love them.

Sam exhibited no obvious signs of mental illness during his two decades of life, nor had he really asked for help in that way. So, it was a heartbreaking tragedy and terrible surprise when Sam

Gawel took his own life. He was twenty-one years old—a kid from our community, from our congregation, from our family.

While we say that Sam "took his own life," the truth is that mental illness killed Sam in the same way cancer or heart attacks kill. Sam's brain malfunctioned, misfired. It seems to me, though, that it wasn't mental illness alone that killed Sam. Millions of people live with mental illness and it doesn't take their lives. But hopelessness is a comorbidity for those with mental illness, and hopelessness mixed with mental illness can kill. I fear that there is a culture of doom overtaking our society, perpetuated by television pundits, culture warriors, and politicians exploiting our fears. This culture of doom combined with an undisclosed mental illness is what took away my friend Sam and far too many others as well.

There exists a heaviness to the world around us. We are confronting a litany of challenges and obstacles, a laundry list of evil doers and hate-mongers. Though the data tells us that people around the world are more literate, more vaccinated, healthier, safer, and less impoverished than ever in history, it nevertheless feels in many ways like we are nearing a tipping point toward disaster. When social media and our overconsumption of the 24/7 news cycle amplify stories of suffering and warnings about worst-case scenarios, the hopelessness becomes contagious. Hopelessness is spreading, and left unchecked, hopelessness threatens to overtake our world.

But as believers, we are uniquely qualified to battle hopelessness because at the center of everything our faith stands for is hope. Religion demands that we give hope to the hopeless and that we internalize hopefulness ourselves, because our faith reminds us that just as free will leads to evil, so too can free will lead to blessing. So, in Sam's memory, I am asking you to join me in choosing to hope and in becoming a source of hopefulness.

Out of Egypt and Back to Egypt[1]

The twenty-first century is hardly the first with great challenges, and human history might suggest as warranted a certain degree of pessimism. Indeed, Genesis tells us that evil has been with us since day six, when God created humans. Adam and Eve abused their free will by eating the fruit from the tree of knowledge of good and evil—the one thing God asked them not to do. Then, one generation later, Cain killed Abel and had the chutzpah to ask God, "Am I my brother's keeper?" Because of human free will, violence and jealousy, lies and selfishness entered the world. We are exiled from God's presence: like a parent utterly repulsed by her children's choices, God required that we leave the "nest" and try to fly on our own.

In fact, the Israelites' descent into exile began with their own senseless hatred of brothers against brothers.[2] As we know, Joseph's brothers were jealous of their father's special love for Joseph, and they were jealous of Joseph's dreams of his own greatness, so the brothers threw Joseph in a pit and left him for dead. Eventually Joseph was found by nomads who brought him down to Egypt and sold him there in Egypt into servitude. Joseph ascended to great heights as his dreams predicted, and Joseph guided Pharaoh to use the seven years of plenty to save for the seven years of famine that ravaged the Middle East. Seeing the riches of Egypt, Joseph's brothers fled from the Holy Land to escape the famine, and their descent into Egypt planted the seeds for centuries of suffering and slavery at the hands of Pharaoh. The Israelites' exile into Egypt began when family members failed to care for each other.

Allow me to fast forward nearly one thousand years. During that millennium, God brought the nation of Israel out of Egypt and returned us to the promised land. We came to govern ourselves and we built a holy temple. God allowed us to thrive again in the land of Israel. But we strayed from the path, worshiping idols

---

1. Gratitude to my teacher Dr. Micah Goodman for sharing this perspective with me.

2. Rashi on Exod 2:13–14.

and perhaps even worse, like the children of Jacob, our ancestors failed to love their neighbor as themselves.

In those times, like today, Israel was in a tough neighborhood. The Jews failed to pay their protection money to the area bully, also known as the Babylonians. In addition, and perhaps even worse, they descended into civil war. And so it was, the Bible tells us, that some 2,500 years ago, the mighty King Nebuchadnezzar of Babylonia moved against Jerusalem. He besieged the city until the famine left the city's residents in starvation. The walls were breached and the Judean King Zedekiah captured by our enemies. The Judean leadership was exiled to Babylonia and the house of the ETERNAL in Jerusalem destroyed (2 Kgs 25).

The Babylonians then named a Jewish governor—Gedalyah—to lead the defeated remnant of Israel. A plot was hatched, and during a state dinner, a cousin of the deposed Jewish king assassinated Gedalyah: one Jew murdered another Jew. Like in the days of Joseph, the Jews had turned against each other. When fighting occurs within families, the entire Jewish people suffers for generations.

After killing the Jewish governor, the Jewish assassin and his followers fled and found their way down to Egypt for safety. To summarize, then, the entirety of biblical history: we came out of Egypt only to go right back to Egypt. The dark side of human free will—jealousy and violence, power and conflict—brought us out of Israel and into Egypt during the days of Joseph. Jealousy and violence caused our time in Israel to come to an end during the days of the Babylonians. From the great heights of self-sovereignty, we descended again to become a people exiled and oppressed: an inglorious end to biblical history. Truly, "from Egypt and back to Egypt" offers us a pessimistic understanding of the human condition, and I must admit at times it feels like despite the great strides of progress and modernity, we continue to live with immorality, with instability, and with intolerance.

That said, few of us would probably define ourselves as hopeless, but the language we use around each other and especially around our kids and grandchildren certainly evokes a palpable despair, as if our entire way of life is terminal. Power-hungry politicians play off our fears and stoke our anger. The cable news pundits we watch and the op-ed writers we read pollute our hearts and minds with their vitriol. For some reason, we tolerate this poisoning of our national dialogue, and we repeat their over-simplified sound bites in conversation and on social media. Certainly, our world has significant and serious problems, and we are obligated to address them. However, when we use language or accept language that is hyperinflammatory, polarizing, and doomsday, then we contribute to hopelessness. Proverbs 18:21 teaches, "Death and life are in the power of the tongue."

Optimism Requires Human Agency

Yet even with the biblical warning about human abuses of free will, the Bible is ultimately a purveyor of hope. Our most central text tells us that when we cease our indifference to human suffering—that when we act with simple kindness toward another person—we can with God's help bring our own salvation.

The children of Jacob lingered in exile in Egypt for four centuries, suffering oppression and enslavement. Their hope was seemingly lost when Pharaoh issued the worse decree of all: fearing that the Hebrews would war against him, Pharaoh required the murder of all baby boys born to the Israelites. Two women, however, refused to accede to this wicked command. Two women recognized their duty to usher life into this world, rather than snuff it out. Jewish tradition identifies these two midwives as Yocheved and Miriam, though the text of scripture refers to them by the Egyptian names Shifrah and Puah. What is clear is that the seeds of the Israelites' redemption from Egypt were planted by these two righteous women, and in so doing, they gave hope to a people otherwise hopeless.

Then, in trying to understand why God finally redeemed the Israelites after centuries of slavery, one ancient biblical commentator taught that the Hebrews continued to linger in slavery in Egypt until God saw that the radical acts of compassion initiated by those two midwives began to spread to the people. When one person finished making his own quota of bricks, he then turned to help a weaker neighbor. Others followed suit. The seeds of redemption were watered when one person performed a small act of kindness toward another.[3]

Redemption bloomed when Moses saw an Egyptian abusing an Israelite, and Moses rose in the Israelite's defense. When you save one life, it is as if you save the world.[4] The combination of our ancestors acting compassionately toward each other with Moses's act of justice and protection caused the garden of redemption to spring forth. Exile commences from sibling strife, but redemption begins when siblings stand together. Exile is rooted in human indifference to the suffering of others, but redemption commences when humans take even small steps toward healing the wounds of another person. There is hope when we care for each other in kindness.

Hope as a Choice

A central message of faith is that we can turn from our selfishness and from our cynicism to give hope to the hopeless and to accept hopefulness ourselves. Rooted in our relationship with a forgiving, compassionate Heavenly Parent, the foundation of hope is the human ability to recognize our mistakes and shortcomings and to change. Rooted in our desire to emulate the Holy One, the foundation of hope is the desire to actively show others that positive change can occur.

I wish that my friend Sam Gawel, and people suffering from hopelessness like Sam, could ask for and receive the help they need. I wish they could really behold the profound goodness in the world that I see every day. I wish they could see those who give so fully of themselves to the poor, the hungry, the suffering. I wish they—I wish Sam—could count the hundreds upon hundreds of

3. Lieber and Harlow, *Etz Hayim*, 326.
4. b. Sanh. 37a.

people comforting each other and comforting Sam's family because of the tremendous amount of love that exists in this world.

There is so much love, goodness, and kindness in this world. I am deeply, deeply hopeful about the future of humanity because I see how much hope we can provide through our actions. And not just I but also Sam's family—even in the midst of all this—wants the world to know of their hope for the future because they too see the good works being done. We must speak of our hope and we must continue to provide hope. We must spread word about all the reasons to hope and we must bring the hope to reality. We must; for the sake of our children, our community, our people . . . we must.

The Hebrew Bible reminds us that just as free will leads to evil, so too can free will lead to blessing. So, in memory of Sam and all who, like Sam, lost their hope, I am asking you to join me in rejecting the language of despair and derision. God is pleading with us to choose hope and to perpetuate hopefulness with our words, for sure, and especially by performing small acts of kindness for those who are in need. In turn, we call on God to nourish and to nurture our hope, and then we will work to spread hope to all who need. Hope is a product of our adult relationship with God. Hope is one of the benefits of remembering to call home.

12

Joyful Are Those Who Seek God

In addition to hope, what are some of the other benefits of re-membering to call home?

Perhaps there has been in history no question more asked than, "What is the meaning of life?" We look around the world and we see gladness and joy, but also suffering and pain. We wonder why some prosper and others suffer, and we are especially concerned when those who are "evil" prosper and those who are "good" suffer. We look at ourselves and we wonder why *we* are here, on Earth, at this moment in time. What are we "to do"? What is our role? Are we—our minds, bodies, and souls—simply the product of a chance meeting between a sperm and an egg, or is there something more to our existence?

I attended a funeral many years ago where the deceased was eulogized with a poem that, if it truly summarized the total of the deceased's raison d'être, described a life poorly lived. The poem suggests, "Life should not be a journey to the grave with the intention of arriving safely in a pretty and well preserved body, but rather to skid in broadside in a cloud of smoke, thoroughly used up, totally worn out, and loudly proclaiming, 'Wow! What a

Ride!'"[1] I heard this and I thought, can *this* really be the meaning of life? And that experience, combined with both attending and officiating memorial services (most of which, by the way, were fitting tributes to beloved family members), led me on my own journey to explore what I believe is truly a sacred question: What is the meaning of life?

The Meaning of Life

Given my chosen career path, it is probably no surprise that my search for the meaning of life started first with the best-selling book of all time: the Bible. And where better to start in the Bible than, well, Genesis. "When God began to create the heaven and earth, the earth chaotic and unorganized with darkness over the surface of the deep and a wind from God sweeping over the water, God said, 'Let there be light'; and there was light. God saw that the light was good, and God separated the light from the darkness. God called the light 'day,' and the darkness God called 'night.' There was evening and there was morning, day one" (Gen 1:1-5). In other words, God's most important act was not creation per se, but rather the act of bringing organization to the chaos. God took that which was seemingly random, full of disorder, and made it "good."

So, if humans are created in the image of God (Gen 1:27), we might conclude that perhaps the meaning of life—our role on this earth—is to be like God: that is, we are to act like the One who brings "order" to the "chaos." But what does it mean to bring "order" to the "chaos"? Is it our own individual chaos or global chaos? What is "order" and how do we bring it?

Another biblical source that offers us a prescription for the meaning of life is the prophet Micah (6:8) who teaches, "What is it that God wants of us? Only to do justice, to love mercy, and to walk humbly with your God." Interestingly Isaiah seemingly counters Micah's three statements regarding the purpose of existence, declaring—as it were—I can summarize the purpose in two!

1. Thompson, "Life Should Not Be." This quotation is attributed to both Hunter Thompson and Matthew Fitzgerald.

"Keep justice and do righteousness" (Isa 56:1). But then comes the prophet Amos who seemingly shouts, "God wants three things of us? Two? No . . . just one thing!" Amos, speaking in God's voice, challenges us, "Seek me and you shall live" (Amos 5:4). If we seek God, then, apparently, we are living the life that God wants of us.

Finding Meaning in the Search

We all have heard of those who believe that *finding* God is the solution to many of life's problems; that it is *finding* God that leads to joy. Of course, there is a certain sense of irony to the expression. Is God lost that God needs to be found? Or, perhaps it is not God who is lost, but us! As the old spiritual goes, "I once was lost, but now I'm found, was blind but now I see!" In his own day, King David accepted the same concept—that is to say, it is not "finding" God that matters but seeking God. Among David's most notable accomplishments is his establishment of Jerusalem as the capital of the ancient kingdom of Israel. When the king celebrated the ark of the covenant's arrival in what was to become the City of Gold, David was so moved that he cried out in excitement, "Let the heart of all who seek the ETERNAL rejoice" (1 Chr 16:10). The same sentiment is recorded in Psalm 105:3. "Let the heart of all who seek the ETERNAL rejoice." In both verses, the operative word is "seek." But what does that mean for us in the twenty-first century? *How* do we seek God? *Where* do we seek God? *When* do we seek God? And, perhaps most importantly, *why* do we seek God?

I was in the potato chip aisle of the local supermarket. I was looking for Pringles (I really like Pringles) but he was looking at my *keepah* (yarmulke). An older man in torn blue jeans and a wrinkled shirt, he walked up to me. "You're Jewish, right?" I nodded hesitantly, wondering silently if this was the beginning of an anti-Semitic event. "They say you're God's chosen people, right?" I told him, somewhat reluctantly, that "yes," this is what the Bible says. I wasn't sure what to do next. After all, I was stuck between potato chip bags and bottles of soda pop. The man grabbed my arm, and I grew even more alarmed. I looked deep into his eyes . . . and he started crying. "My wife is sick," he told me. "And we don't have any money. I don't want no charity, but I left church a long time ago and never went back. I just need someone to pray for me and, well, you're God's chosen people." And so I did, right there in the potato chip aisle: I prayed for him and his wife with all my heart and soul.

And that was that. He went his way; I went mine. What was fascinating to me was not that he wanted to pray, nor even that he identified me as a religious person. I was a little surprised that he sought God in the potato chip aisle. I guess if I were looking for God I would probably head toward the baked goods or the chicken soup, but I suppose that comes from growing up Jewish. What fascinated me most, though, was this large man's recognition that he had no control over his wife's illness. There was nothing left for him to do but to pray and to rely on God for help.

In times of crisis, many of us are pretty good about seeking God—sometimes even in the potato chip aisle of a local grocery store. At one point or another, each of us stands face-to-face with our own mortality and that of those whom we love. In those moments, we feel like only God is in control; we often pray for a miracle. Usually, though, if that miracle comes, it arrives in the form of the kindness or wisdom of another: the doctor or nurse who identifies the health crisis and can fix it; the loving soul who offers an extended hand or a listening heart. So we are told, "You shall love your neighbor as (you love) yourself" (Lev 19:18), and we are reminded to "walk in God's ways" (Deut 30:16). If and when we can bring help and healing to another person, we are obligated to do so. We are toward each other *in loco Parentis*.

At the same time, like adult children who look toward Mom or Dad and know that everything will be okay because our parents have our backs, we likewise put our faith in God and hope that everything will be okay. When we call home, we receive the reassurance we need to continue taking steps forward. When we seek God, we can live our best lives.

Searching with a Map

My wife, Rebecca, and I traveled with my in-laws to Hawaii in
2007. It was our last big adventure before our first child, Caleb,
came along. Rebecca was, at the time, about five months pregnant.
One day on our vacation we decided to take our chances at the
Pineapple Garden Maze on the Dole Plantation (Oahu): "officially"
recognized in the *Guinness Book of World Records 2001* as the
world's largest maze. Covering an area of three acres with a path
length of 3.11 miles, it was at least at the time made of 11,400 colorful Hawaiian plants, including varieties of hibiscus, the official
state flower. Don't worry: I didn't count them. I'm just reporting
what the brochure said.

The Dole Plantation was absolutely beautiful, but the maze
was impossible! We had no way of knowing which paths led further in and which led further out, since to us they all looked the
same. After more than an hour of toiling endlessly, I decided to
walk right through all the bushes until we found the end. This certainly was not in keeping to the rules, mind you, but Rebecca was
five months pregnant and *very* hungry and . . . well, you get the
picture. As we were leaving, I couldn't help but think there should
be two options for this maze: 1) the traditional maze approach of
trial and error and 2) a map provided so that we could enjoy the
beautiful flowers and pathways while weaving our way from beginning to end. And then I could have really enjoyed the 11,400
colorful Hawaiian plants *and* I could've found lunch for Rebecca
at a reasonable hour.

While the Dole Plantation Maze did not provide us with options, God has. As Rabbi Moshe Chaim Luzzatto taught a couple
centuries ago, life is just such a maze. We have the option of following life's paths blindly, hoping to get lucky and to discover
meaning and purpose along the way—all the while knowing the
great potential for failure and directionless wandering. Or we have
another option: to follow the "map" that gives us form, structure,
and meaning on our journey—the map that allows us to enjoy the
beautiful flowers and pathways, weaving our way from beginning

to end. That map, says Rabbi Luzzatto, is the Bible.[2] "Align the course of your feet," the book of Proverbs (4:26) tells us, "and all your ways will prosper." In the path laid out for us to emulate God and to follow God's laws, we have been given the road map so that we might live a life of meaning, of purpose, and of partnership with the Divine. It is not God who is lost that God must somehow "be found"; we humans are the ones, too often, who are lost. And, in the same way we seek the way out of a maze, so ought we to find our way back to the Holy One.

In calling out to our people thousands of years ago, the prophet Isaiah (51:1–3) declared, "Listen to me, you pursuers of righteousness *and seekers of the ETERNAL*; look to the rock from where you have been cut, and to the hole of the pit from where you have been dug. Look to Abraham your father, and to Sarah who gave birth to you . . . For the ETERNAL shall comfort Zion; [God] will comfort all her ruins; and [God] will make her wilderness like Eden, and her desert like the garden of the ETERNAL; joy and gladness shall be found in there, thanksgiving, and the voice of melody." In seeking God, in being like Abraham and Sarah who left everything they knew to build a relationship with their Creator, we will find comfort. We will find joy and gladness. And there we will find thanksgiving and the voice of melody. "Let the heart of all who seek the ETERNAL rejoice," David told us (1 Chr 16:10). And all we have to do to seek; all we have to do is to pick up the phone.

2. Luzzatto, *Mesilat Yesharim*.

13

Honoring Our Parents,
Honoring God

"I AM STARTING TO write today, because of my age. I am now 84 years old," my grandfather wrote to his family in 2004. "I went through a lot during those years [of the Holocaust]. I remember a lot from my younger years. I know I will not be here forever. I would like my children, grandchildren, and great-grandchildren to know a little about my life. I will try to write everything to my best recollection. I want my children and everybody who reads this autobiography to know that everything in it is true."

So begins the unpublished autobiography of my grandfather, Wolf Gruca, a concentration camp survivor from Poland who, in 2021, died at age 101. For several years we had been encouraging my grandfather to tell us more about his childhood and what happened to him during the Holocaust. My grandmother passed away in 2000, and with her went many untold stories. So it was with great excitement and relief that I found out that my grandfather decided to write his life story.

While his story is unique, it is inextricably bound with the eternal narrative of the Jewish people. I set out encouraging

Grandpa to write a history. The result: my grandfather's autobiography, like many of our parents' and grandparents' stories, as well as the Bible, is more about memory than history. It is more about the experiences that find a place in our hearts than about the specific places, times, and events that drift easily into and out of one's mind. Wolf Gruca's autobiography does not mean to teach us about a history of the twentieth century. Rather it reminds us that, when all is said and done, what we will remember is the love of our parents, our love for our children, and the kind acts performed for us by others. When all is said and done, what truly matters are the moments we spent together and the memories we share.

Unlike the rest of the animal world, we humans crave a sense of history; more than that, though, we yearn for an understanding of our world. We know where we are today, but we wonder how we got here. This need for understanding history is ancient. Our Bible is—in some part—an attempt to provide such a history. Assembled by Jews living in Israel more than two thousand years ago, the Bible represents a collection of stories that essentially answers the question "how did we get to where we are today?" It is this question, "how did we get to where we are today?" that initially drove us to ask my grandfather for his autobiography.

"I was the youngest in the house," Grandpa wrote, with his fractured English sometimes coming through the written text; I can even hear his heavy Polish accent as I read it. "My name is Wolf. My father had three brothers and one sister: all who were married and had families. My mother had four brothers and one sister, also; all were married and had families. When I could count all the relatives from both families, I would say there were between sixty and seventy members. Most of the relatives the Germans sent to the gas chambers."

My grandfather goes on to recount being forced into the Czestochowa ghetto where two of his brothers died fighting the Germans. He tells about being sent as slave labor to the Hasag-Pelzer factory. From there the Germans took him from one concentration camp to another: Buchenwald, Dora, and Osterode am Harz. His autobiography tells us about a death march, about how he navigated his way through war-torn Germany to an American DP camp, and then how he, my grandmother, and my then-infant uncle found refuge in the United States. For me, this history answered the basic question "how did we get to where we are today?" just like the biblical books of Joshua, Judges, Samuel, Kings, and Chronicles represent a collection of stories that attempted to answer the same question for our ancestors.

However, sacred texts seek to do more than simply relate history or memory; they attempt to explain the meaning behind those events. These sacred texts also offer a prescription for living that embraces our collective memory and the significance behind it. Repeatedly we are told of the Israelites' sufferings at the hands of the Egyptians, of God's saving power in redeeming us—not as an abstract history lesson, but so that we remember the role that God plays in our lives and so that we are inspired to act like God when we can play that role in others' lives. The Bible teaches us that, because of our memory of Egypt, we have an obligation to help others as well.

My grandfather wrote,

> I would like to tell you a story about a name that I will never forget for the rest of my life. This happened two or three years before the war started. I was teenager, and I remember this name like this incident happened today. My father (may he rest in peace) started to become sick. He went to a lot of doctors that practice in our city in each of the two hospitals. None of the doctors could tell what was wrong with my father. My mother, rest in peace, went with my father to Krakow University in Poland, which had one of the largest hospitals. Even there, none of the doctors could diagnose what was wrong with my father. After two weeks my father and mother came back home, and the doctors told my mother to watch out because soon my father's life would come to an end. Day by day, my father's health went downhill, 'til one day my uncle thought he was dead. My uncle had already lit candles for my father. At the same time, a cousin of my father's, who was from a different section of the city, was visiting my

dying father. She told us that a new doctor from Russia came to the city.

I remember like it was yesterday. My two brothers ran to this doctor and begged him to come to see our father. He said he would come as long as we provided and paid for a horse and buggy to bring him to our house and to take him back home. We provided his wishes. After a few minutes with my father the doctor came out and said that if my father could live through the night, he would come back the next morning with a surgeon and reexamine my father. The next morning the doctor and surgeon came and examined my father. They opened the door to my father's room and asked for a dish. My older brother, Shlomo, grabbed a dish, which in the Jewish home we used to wash our hands with. The dish had two handles and we gave it to the doctors. When the doctors came out of the room, the dish was full of blood and water. They never told us where this blood was taken from. When the doctors left and the family went in to see our father, we could see a different person. In the first few days we could see a lot of improvement. It took a year for my father to return to his full health. The name of the doctor was Dr. Blagowidow. The name of the surgeon was Dr. Mikulski. After this miracle the whole neighborhood took them for their doctors.

As this story demonstrates and as our sacred scriptures demand, we remember the kind acts done for us by others, and we use these memories as motivation to practice such deeds in return.

Even more to the point, our strongest memories are created by those whom we love: our family and friends. Of course, for most of us, those are healthy relationships. When our children grow up, they will not remember scores from little league baseball; they will remember whether we helped to coach the teams. Our children might not remember the errands they ran with us, but they will certainly remember the Sabbath and holiday meals with family and friends. When our children grow up, they might not even remember every detail about Sunday school; but they will remember whether we walked them to class, whether they saw us at prayer alongside them, and whether we as adults continue to study our religion and serve as models of the importance of lifelong learning.

Here is how Grandpa began his autobiography:

> First I would like to acknowledge my parents, because everybody has good parents, but I had special parents. . . . My parents did a lot of things especially for me because I did not eat dairy. They would buy special, for me, a piece of herring, sour pickles, salami, or smoked fish, all of which were luxuries in Europe before the war. When I did not have these special foods, all I ate during the day was dry bread or bread with a little bit of chicken or goose fat spread on it. . . .
>
> When I finished public school, my parents sent me to learn a trade. I remember what I ate from morning 'til I came home from school, day after day five days a week. In the house next to us lived a baker whose name was Lazer Stern, a man with a long beard. I went into his bakery every day and he gave me one Kaiser roll and a piece of cake. . . . My parents paid up every week for my Kaiser roll and a piece of cake.

From Gratitude to Action

Unlike my grandfather, we have a little less appreciation for the piece of herring or bread with chicken fat on it. But we remember the times our parents went out of their way for us. We remember when our parents put forth that extra effort to be with us or to be there for us. So too does Deuteronomy instruct us the same way to remember what God did for us in days of old: how God brought us out of Egypt with a mighty hand and an outstretched arm. We remember; we give thanks; and we desire to act in such a way as to make our parents proud.

At eighty-four years old, reflecting on his life, my grandfather wrote nothing about the forty years he put in at the Chrysler assembly plant. He wrote little about the horrors of World War II or how he came from Poland to Germany to America. Instead, he wrote about the love of his parents; he wrote about his love for his children; and he wrote about the people who went above and beyond by performing acts of true kindness toward them. What will our children write about when they are eighty-four? What will we write about? Not about the sixty hours a week we put in at work. Not about the house, or the car, or the bills that often dominate our minds. We and our children will write about the time spent together at that synagogue or church, at baseball or around the family table. We will write about holiday dinners with family and close friends. We will write about our rabbi or pastor and the friendships made within our holy communities. We will write about that one television show we always watched together with our parents or with our children. And we will write about how we took some time to help those in need, and how others did the same for us.

Among the blessings of faith is the opportunity to interweave the timely with the timeless. In the moment, we enjoy beautiful relationships with those closest to us. We also recognize how those moments impact the generations. In the moment, however, we sometimes struggle to enjoy or to appreciate every small act of kindness we perform toward someone in need. Nevertheless, we know that, in embracing the sacred obligation of caring for those people, such efforts make a difference over the long run. When we strive to act in such a way as to bring honor to our family name—whether for our parents' sake, our children's sake, or our own—when we perform acts of loving-kindness for those who are in need the same way that our parents lovingly cared for us, then, through the respectful act of emulation, we as adult children deepen our relationships with those who came before and with God on high.

For those of us who are parents, and for each of us who is someone's child, we affirm the role of the parent as the rule-maker and disciplinarian, but also as the one who kisses boo-boos and tucks children in with a hug and a bedtime story at the end of the day. But you can't have one without the other. We have all witnessed undisciplined children who yell when they should whisper and run when they should walk, but whom their mom or dad never corrects. I have watched enough of those *Supernanny* shows on TV to know this is true . . . and disastrous. But we have also seen children who are over-disciplined, missing out on the warmth of a parent's embrace. Parents have the awesome responsibility of trying to balance discipline and compassion, justice, and mercy—all in the name of loving their children.

The Bible places great importance on the relationship between parents and children. Twice the Ten Commandments tell us to honor our father and mother (Exod 20:12 and Deut 5:16), and once to revere our mother and father (Lev 19:3). In addition, the sages of old enumerate the responsibilities of a parent toward a child, and in Judaism, at each Friday night meal, Jewish parents bless their children. Equally, our sages instruct us as children of all ages on how to fulfill the commandment of honoring our mother and father. For example, we show honor by standing up whenever one of our parents, grandparents, or even teachers enter the room: we rise in their presence. Moreover, when we engage in prayer, sacred study, or acts of loving-kindness, we stand on the shoulders of those who came before us.

Among the most important lessons our parents taught us is how we treat other people, and upon this many of us focus exclusively. Have we given enough to charitable causes? Have we fought for the rights of the poor and oppressed? Have we stood up to hatred, bigotry, and prejudice? Have we fed the hungry and clothed the naked? When we are stopped at a red light and a person is there asking for a few dollars, do we reach into our pockets to offer that person some money or a granola bar or bottle of water we might keep on hand for just such a purpose? We wonder, "Have I acted in a way that would make my parents proud?"

No matter how old we get, how learned or wise we become, we remember the sound of our parents' voices and the expressions on their faces when we help a friend or when we fail to do so. The ethical lessons our parents teach us are rooted in the Bible and are central to our never-ending struggle to become a holy nation of good, decent individuals: Don't kill. Don't steal. Don't withhold pay from an employee. Love your neighbor as yourself. Yet, these principles are also found in the notes written on napkins tucked into lunch bags that say, simply, "Be good today" or "Say something nice to a friend." They are reflected in conversations around the dinner table when parents ask about their child's day at school or about a friend's well-being; and these ethical principles are reinforced at times when a mother makes her child sit down to watch *The Oprah Winfrey Show* with her because Oprah is talking about teens and sex, or children who smoke, or abusive relationships, or anything else that Mom feels is an important parent-child conversation and that Oprah is a good vehicle for those discussions. Oops, maybe that last one about Oprah was just my mom and me.

These lessons taught to us by our parents are meant to serve us throughout our life and, perhaps intentionally or unintentionally, these same ethics remind us of our obligations toward our parents as they begin to age. Without doubt, each of us honors our parents when we treat others with kindness and when we try to make the world a better place. But imagine if, as children, we never once said thank you to mom or dad for a good meal or for a new toy. Imagine if, as adults, we stopped visiting our parents or calling them, if we never joined them for dinner or invited them to a celebration, or if, when their time comes, we never visited their grave. We do it out of appreciation for our parents, out of love, out of respect, out of a desire to fulfill the commandment to honor our father and our mother—and we always do it with humility.

Likewise, when we are at prayer, we look even beyond the expectations of our earthly parents to stand before our Heavenly Parent. We reflect on the choices we have made and will make, grateful for God's presence in our lives during the difficult moments, like a parent who holds us and says that everything will be alright. We remember that, like a parent, God balances discipline and compassion, justice, and mercy—all in the name of loving us, God's children.

We gather in our houses of worship to reflect on how successful we were in following God's laws, set forth like a parent would: out of love and compassion. And, like the commandments regarding interpersonal behavior, our sacred Scripture provides for us lessons on our relationship with God.

We know how to show our respect for our parents. We act justly, like they taught us; we behave compassionately, like they taught us; we rise when they walk in a room; we say "thank you"; we visit, we call; we join them for dinner occasionally; we invite them to share with us in celebrations. We tolerate constructive nagging; we put up with their bad jokes and we speak at the top of our lungs so they can hear us; we recite memorial prayers. And we do it because it's the right thing to do.

But how, then, do we show our similar respect for our Heavenly Parent? Just as we might honor a parent by cooking Mom or Dad a favorite meal, so too do we show our love for God by engaging in prayer, by studying and teaching scripture to our children, and by making blessings over our food. Just as we honor another parent when we—consciously or not—wash our cars just the way that parent taught us, so too do we honor God by engaging in holiday celebrations, by participating faithfully in religious life cycle ceremonies, and by showing deference to our faith traditions. Additionally, how many of us would love to take a ten-year sabbatical from work to eat good food, to drink good wine, to rest, and to spend time with our family? By honoring God through a lifetime of Sabbath observance, each of us can enjoy such a sabbatical, just in one-day-a-week increments.

From Rocking Chair to Rock of Ages

As a child, I possessed quite an overactive imagination and thus struggled to fall asleep. I clearly remember my childhood nighttime rituals. First, my parents read to me the book *Mr. Happy* by Roger Hargreaves. Then they lifted me up and together we looked out the window to go through all the children on the block who were going to sleep: "Marty is asleep," we would whisper together. "Tommy is asleep. Stephanie is asleep." And so on. Then they tucked me into bed, kissed me, and my dad chanted with singsong in Yiddish, Hebrew, and English for me to "make it a good night sleep." They turned out the lights and left the room.

No more than thirty seconds after they exited, I took the pillows on my bed and built them into a wall between the window and me. After all, I figured, if someone were to break in, surely they would not see me behind this wall of pillows! Five minutes would pass, and, at this point, I would have so freaked myself out about a burglar breaking in that I would leave my bedroom to tell my parents that I could not sleep. So, each time, my father would pick me up and sit us down in this rickety old wooden rocking chair. Then, my dad would rock us, back and forth, back and forth—me on dad's lap and his arms around me, as together we counted each rock until we hit sixty. At sixty, I knew it was time to go back to bed, and sure enough, I was asleep often even before my head hit the pillow.

Another childhood memory. I used to tease my mom about how short she is. That is not very nice, I know, but my mom is short, and it did not take long before I was taller than she is. Rather than respond with anger whenever I teased her, my mom would simply say, "No matter how big you get, you will always be my baby." We look back on these memories fondly now, and many of us have similar memories as a child or as a parent. But more than just memories, these experiences serve as a paradigm for my relationship with God. Whenever I am sad, scared, or hurting, I feel God embracing me as we rock on that rickety old wooden rocking chair, back and forth, back and forth, counting to sixty. Whenever I am feeling arrogant or head strong, I picture God telling me, "No matter how big you get, you will always be my baby." So it is with our parents, and so it is with God too.

The Bible instructs us to hold sacred the relationship between parents and children. The commandments demand that parent and child each takes care of the other and, in turn, we remember God in the process. From that model of mutual care that God showed the Israelites, and that parents and children are instructed to show each other, all of us are commanded to reach out to the poor and needy, to the sick and old, to our faith community, and to the strangers who dwell among us. When we fulfill the commandments regarding interpersonal behavior, we honor our parents, and we honor God. Moreover, when we fulfill the sacred obligations required of us in our relationship with God, so too do we show our love and respect to all our parents: those on this earth, those in the spirit world, and to our Heavenly Parent, God above. In these ways—among other ways—are how, as adults, we begin to call home.

14

Don't Forget to Call Home

IN OUR FAMILY, BUYING gifts for our parents is terribly difficult. Thank God, they have everything they need and most of what they want. When we were kids and probably even more now that we are adults, our parents want from us the gifts of time and relationships. We welcome them into our lives, sharing our ups and downs. We ask for advice. We include them in our children's journeys, and we ask for their help in raising our kids. We invite them over for meals and we go to ball games with them. We let them see us happy and we thank them for helping to make us this way. Every day, we call home. Our parents cannot solve every problem for us, but they can support us through their love, and we can support them through our love.

Likewise, God might be perceived as an empty-nester Parent. God will not solve every problem we have, but God wants a little of our time and God wants all of us our love. Most of all, God wants us to follow God's lead: to act with compassion and to pursue justice. And in turn, God will show us God's love. God will do so, that is, as long we don't forget to call home.

A Metaphor

Of course, the image of God as our empty-nester Parent is just a metaphor, and all analogies are imperfect. Like Job, we cannot fully understand God's ways, but we know that there is strength and meaning in faith. When times are at their most desperate, we want and perhaps even need to believe in a God who acts. We want and perhaps even need to believe that God will send a miracle, however small or large that miracle needs to be. So, in those moments, perhaps we are best to listen to the advice of baseball great Satchel Page, who reminds us, "Don't pray when it rains if you don't pray when the sun shines."[1] We must acknowledge God in the good times as much as in the difficult times. And, truly, in those most difficult moments, I hope our prayers come true. In the most difficult moments, I pray to God, and I hope that, like a parent caring for a young child, God acts when we need God to act.

That said, the idea of a God who rewards the righteous with blessings and punishes the sinners is challenged by most of our lived reality. Far too often we see the wicked prosper and the good suffer. Additionally, to accept that suffering is meant as some sort of lesson for the sufferer or for others is a challenging justification, especially when we confront the suffering of children. As perhaps the lowest period in human history, the Holocaust calls the entire belief system of blessings and curses into question. Sometimes, God does not grant us the miracle for which we prayed, and it is not a reflection of our righteousness. Moreover, our suffering, while it might come to teach lessons to us or to others, cannot be justified by the fact that learning occurs. Certainly, in those moments in which suffering occurs, perhaps God is answering our prayer in a different way, and God knows better than we do what we need. The Bible certainly suggests that God intercedes directly in human affairs, even if we cannot understand God's motives or ways.

Perhaps, though, perhaps the world simply behaves the way it behaves because, at this point in history, God is our empty-nester Parent waiting on us to act. After raising the human race from

---

1. Quoted in Donadio et al., *New York Public Library Book*, 357.

infancy through childhood and then into the teenage stage, God is now waiting on us as adults to act with gratitude, obligation, joy, and hope. God is waiting on us to act like the adults we are. God wants us to use the free will that God has gifted us.

For Grandpa

Grandpa, I don't really understand how God could allow the Holocaust to happen. I don't really understand how God allows any suffering to occur. But when I look at the countless acts of kindness inspired by believers, then I am inspired to believe. When I see the family that you helped to build, how you arrived in America with next to nothing materially and with a wife and baby for whom to care, and when I see all that you built, then, frankly, I believe that God's hand is quietly at work. When I see what my parents helped to build, that which my wife and I are trying to build, and all that our extended family has built, then I feel God's love the same way that I felt and continue to feel your love. And, with the State of Israel thriving in so many ways despite the incredible obstacles stacked against it, I believe that, yes, maybe miracles do happen.

Grandpa, when I watched you as a Holocaust survivor holding your great-grandchildren, I couldn't help believing that miracles happen. When I saw you standing next to one of your great-grandsons when he became bar mitzvah, I couldn't help believing that miracles happen.

Then again, at the same time, Grandpa, in celebrating the bar mitzvah of our second son in your absence, we feel your presence and love from a distance the same way that I sometimes perceive God's love: from a distance. Moreover, when I think about the loss you must have felt when so many members of your family were murdered in the Holocaust, Grandpa, then I wonder, maybe God is an empty-nester Parent weeping over human action and inaction.

If we believe in a God who grants us total free will, then we must accept that God will not solve every problem we have. Nevertheless, like an empty-nester Parent, God wants a little of our time and God wants all of our love. Most of all, God wants us to follow God's lead: to express our gratitude; to fulfill our obligations of compassion and justice; to experience joy; and to maintain and perpetuate hope. And in turn, God will show us God's love. God will do so, that is, as long we don't forget to call home.

Bibliography

Cahill, Thomas. *Gift of the Jews*. New York: Anchor, 1998.

Danziger, Lucy, and Catherine Birndorf. *The Nine Rooms of Happiness: Loving Yourself, Finding Your Purpose, and Getting Over Life's Little Imperfections*. New York: Hyperion, 2010.

Donadio, Stephen, et al., eds. *The New York Public Library Book of Twentieth-Century American Quotations*. New York: Warner, 1992.

Harari, Yuval Noah. *Homo Deus*. New York: Vintage, 2016.

Lamm, Norman. "The Face of God." In *Reflections on the Holocaust*, edited by Bernhard H. Rosenberg and Fred Heuman, 136. Jersey City: Ktav, 1991.

Lemonick, Michael. "The Biology of Joy." *Time Magazine*, Jan 17, 2005.

Lieber, David and Jules Harlow. *Etz Hayim Torah and Commentary*. New York: Rabbinical Assembly, 2001.

Luzzatto, Moshe Chaim. *Mesilat Yesharim: The Path of the Just*. Nanuet, NY: Feldheim, 2005.

"The Meaning of True Happiness (Joke)." Masterwordsmith-unplugged (blog), Mar 27, 2009. http://masterwordsmith-unplugged.blogspot.com/2009/03/meaning-of-true-happiness-joke.html.

Morales, Mark and Corky Siemaszko. "Survey Finds That 33 Is the Happiest Age of People's Lives." *Daily News*, Mar 27, 2012. https://www.nydailynews.com/news/survey-finds-33-happiest-age-people-lives-article-1.1051788.

Nagel, Scott. "A Positivity of Happiness in the New Year." Unpublished sermon delivered at Temple Oheb Shalom, Baltimore, MD, Sep 16, 2012.

National Academies of Sciences, Engineering, and Medicine. *Social Isolation and Loneliness in Older Adults: Opportunities for the Health Care System*. Washington, DC: National Academies Press, 2020. https://doi.org/10.17226/25663.

Pausch, Randy, and Jeffrey Zaslow. *The Last Lecture*. New York: Hyperion, 2008.

Rank, Perry Raphael, and Gordon M. Freeman, eds. *Moreh Derech: The Rabbinical Assembly Rabbi's Manual*. New York: Rabbinical Assembly 1998.

Bibliography

Rosling, Hans, et al. *Factfulness: Ten Reasons We're Wrong about the World—And Why Things Are Better than You Think*. New York: Flatiron, 2018.

Sacks, Jonathan. *To Heal a Fractured World: The Ethics of Responsibility*. New York: Schocken, 2007.

Soloveitchik, Joseph. "Kol Dodi Dofek (The Voice of My Beloved Knocks)." In *Reflections on the Holocaust,* edited by Bernhard H. Rosenberg and Fred Heuman, 56. Jersey City: Ktav, 1991.

"Talmud: The William Davidson Edition." Sefaria, n.d. https://www.sefaria.org/texts/Talmud.

Thompson, Hunter S. "Life Should Not Be a Journey to the Grave." Goodreads, n.d. https://www.goodreads.com/quotes/47188-life-should-not-be-a-journey-to-the-grave-with.

"Truthiness." Merriam-Webster, n.d. https://www.merriam-webster.com/dictionary/truthiness.

Wiesel, Elie. *Night*. New York: Hill and Wang, 2006.

Printed in the USA
CPSIA information can be obtained
at www.ICGtesting.com
CBHW050450201023
1420CB00004B/16

9 781666 774405